GRAPHIC DESIGN

problems methods solutions

JERZY KARO

VNR VAN NOSTRAND REINHOLD COMPANY
New York Cincinnati Toronto London Melbourne

To Micha, my wife.

The author and Van Nostrand Reinhold Company have taken all possible care to trace the ownership of every illustration reproduced in this book and to make full acknowledgment for its use. If any errors have accidentally occurred, they will be corrected in subsequent editions, provided notification is sent to the publisher.

Van Nostrand Reinhold Company Regional Offices:
New York Cincinnati Chicago Millbrae Dallas
Van Nostrand Reinhold Company International Offices:
London Toronto Melbourne

Library of Congress Catalog Card Number: 74-6791
ISBN: 0-442-30069-7

Designed by the author

Filmset and printed by Jolly & Barber Ltd, Rugby, Warwickshire

Published by Van Nostrand Reinhold Company Inc.,
450 West 33rd Street, New York N.Y. 10001 and
Van Nostrand Reinhold Company Ltd.,
Molly Millar's Lane, Wokingham, Berks.

16 15 14 13 12 11 10 9 8 7 6 5 4 3 2 1

Library of Congress Cataloging in Publication Data
Karo, Jerzy.
Graphic design : problems, methods, and solutions.
Includes index.
1. Commercial art. 2. Graphic arts – Technique.
I. Title.
NC1000.K37 741.6 74-6791
ISBN 0-442-30069-7

Contents

Foreword	6
Introduction	8
Problem Analysis	11
Methods	14
1. Allegorical	16
2. Direct	25
3. Dramatic	30
4. Emotive	36
5. Illustrative	43
6. Impact	49
7. Implied	54
8. Symbolic	60
9. Typographical	70
10. Unusual	76
11. Whimsical	86
12. Wordless	94
Conclusion	99
Index of Illustrations	102

Foreword

It has been said that language was given to us to express our thoughts, and not to hide them. If such an ideal often seems incompatible with the growing trend of using a meaningless vocabulary to express non-existent ideas, it is because imagination and purpose are required in order to engender creative thought.

In graphics, the creative process is generated by, and particularly concerned with, problems of visual communication. It involves an interest in people, and an understanding of the way they think and feel; an ability for making objective analysis; and the imagination either to create new visual idioms capable of expressing ideas or emotions for which no language as yet exists, or to give new meaning to a phrase long forgotten.

Graphics is an art of purpose. It is the quality of creative thought alone that determines whether it becomes an art in itself.

KARO

Introduction

The underlying basis of most graphic activities and of all aspects of commercial or political advertising is persuasion. To persuade means to prevail on people by advice, urging, reason, inducement etc. to do something . . . to induce to believe, to convince, to influence someone's thoughts or actions. According to desired individual, group, social, or national objectives we are all constantly being prevailed upon, consciously and subconsciously, regardless of race or creed. And of course we are continually attempting to persuade others by whatever means are available, from an unspoken word to legislation. A considerable knowledge of social history is required for one to realize the enormous power and sometimes devastating effects of persuasion. Two isolated but fairly recent historical incidents offer good examples.

The Maji-Maji rebellion of 1905 produced a phenomenon hitherto unsuspected in the East African native – a complete contempt for death in battle. The witch-doctors created a myth that if a warrior and his spear were sprinkled with water from the hot springs of Liwale, he would become immune to the bullets of white oppressors. The natives went into battle certain of immortality, and died in thousands. Yet the apparent failure of the magic did not diminish their faith in it. The witch-doctors' explanation that each fallen warrior must have broken one of the many rules on which this magic depended was entirely accepted.

The other example, of 1939 vintage, has since been widely cited, and incorrectly described as the height of human folly. It refers to those infamous Polish cavalry charges against the German tanks. In the preceding twelve months, the cavalrymen as well as the civilian population were repeatedly told that most of the German tanks were only dummies – tank silhouettes had been made of hardboard, and mounted on motorbikes. The Poles were persuaded to believe this, and they too died. The explanation for the failure of this particular myth was not very different from the one used thirty-four years earlier – the tanks that turned out to real ones happened to be the only few German tanks that *were* real.

So it seems that the question of belief is merely a matter of convincing the majority. After all, how many of our own beliefs are not, in fact, our own? How many of our convictions would survive the light of objective criticism, when even today, in this highly developed and civilized world, we still believe in what is possibly the oldest persuasion gambit – that there's no smoke without fire? Despite the inherent difference of individual characteristics, we have a great many similar habits, many of them acquired during the formative years, and therefore more difficult to give up later on, and practically impossible to change completely. Closer inspection of these habits usually reveals them as not acquired at all, but superimposed by all kinds of human emotions such as prejudice, fear, superstition, envy, ignorance, insecurity, partiality, ambition – and by other people.

Any inveterate beer drinker will readily declare that his loyalty to a specific brand of beer is governed by its taste; but motivational research has discovered that the determining factor is not really the taste, but the image association – that is to say, if the advertising campaign for beer 'X' succeeds in creating a desirable or fashionable image of the man who drinks beer 'X', and if our beer drinker thinks he is that type, or would like to be that type, he will tend to drink beer 'X'. Furthermore, it appears that the in-image of the beer drinker of today is either a rugged out-of-door character, or a sophisticated man-about-town. The rugged type is portrayed as tall, lean, and tough, wearing a pair of irresistible eyes; whereas the sophisticated man-about-town with greying temples is an impeccably attired, cultured, oyster-eating gentleman.

The last two sentences are in themselves an example of persuasion. They clearly imply that the out-of-door character must be rugged, and the gentleman invariably cultured, when in reality a rugged-looking man often turns out to be no more an outdoor character than his opposite number. Neither of them may even drink beer at all – at any rate not with oysters. These built-up images, created and subsequently cultivated by persuasion, nevertheless become widely accepted social opinions.

Each successive generation has always felt a need to emphasize its difference from the previous one. So each new generation seeks and becomes susceptible to the creation of its own image that aims to transform both habits and fashions. This is where a designer needs the skill and ability to translate that new image or language into a visual form, to communicate it, and to ensure its acceptance by the relevant sector of the community.

The success of many advertising campaigns and much political propaganda rests upon our willingness to conform to a particular recognizable pattern of behaviour and lifestyle, which identifies us with some social or professional group to which we belong or aspire. Thus it is ourselves who eventually convert these opinions and images into habits. For our inveterate beer drinker, brand 'X' becomes synonymous with a uniform, club badge, or school tie. He will, quite naturally, tend to respect fellow-beer–'X'-drinkers because he assumes they are like himself, and vice versa.

However there is a significant difference between identification or stimulation of an existing inner ambition to be or do something, and the changing of that desire itself. The former can be relatively simple, and often requires only a subtle nudge of encouragement; whereas the latter is a much more complex problem. To solve problems of this kind demands a highly developed sense of empathy, combined with considerable creative ability. Not only does an old habit have to be broken, but, far more important, a new one must be created in its place, which will involve some personal and social upheaval. At this point one is no longer just a designer, but an emotional catalyst as well.

11

Problem Analysis

Let us imagine that the task is to devise an advertising campaign aimed at persuading our inveterate beer drinker to become a wine drinker instead.

Where does one start? Certainly not in doodling idly – hoping or waiting for inspiration, which seldom, if ever, arrives unaided. Inspiration is the result of thinking, and disciplined thinking at that. If it is too obvious to say that one starts at the beginning, it is still necessary to emphasize that analysis of the problem must always be the starting point, and that the solution of any problem depends on one's degree of understanding of what exactly that problem is. However, disciplined thinking must not be confused with regimented thinking or a stereotyped approach. No two problems are alike, and there are no dull problems – only dull answers. Like people, problems share certain similarities, yet each one has an individual character.

A jig-saw puzzle is an appropriate metaphor in this context, since understanding the nature of the problem, and the inter-relation of its composite parts, is possible only after the separate pieces have all been carefully identified and examined.

The specific problem we are concerned with here poses the following questions:

(1) How should one anticipate and meet the beer drinker's objection or indifference to wine?

(2) What is the reason for that objection or indifference?

(3) What is the character and behavioural code of the social group to which he belongs?

(4) To what social group, if any, does he aspire?

Thus we have four separate but closely interlinked questions, each one involving different emotions:

(a) *Sense of belonging*

Beer is principally consumed in pubs or bars, but pubs are not just drinking places. They are social clubs where one meets one's friends.

(b) *Feeling of security*

To him, the beer drinking fraternity is either an extension of his home, or a desired change from it.

(c) *Fear*

His desire to be associated with a wine drinking set, whatever the motivation, will be tempered by the realization or suspicion that there is more to wine than just drinking it. Wine drinking would also project him into a strange situation, amongst people whose interests and code of social behaviour he doesn't know, or is not used to.

(d) *Prejudice and ignorance*

Any or all of the 'grapes are treaded with bare feet' variety (xenophobia; garlic; pumpernickel; and 'bare feet are dirty feet').

These then are the composite parts, each one apparently posing a different question and needing a separate answer. But do they really? Take this imaginary situation of a man standing under a stopped clock, apparently waiting for someone: (1) *When* 'X' wants to know (2) *Why* the clock has stopped (3) *How* could you tell (4) *What* he is waiting for?

It can be seen that the last question is the most important one, and answers to the others, though they might have some bearing on the situation, will not in themselves tell you what is going on. The answer to the last question will still depend entirely on your own information and experience.

In this situation, then, irrelevant information is sifted out to reveal the essence of the problem.

As regards the questions about the beer drinker, on the other hand, the last one of these is irrelevant, and the first three, which *are* relevant, are clearly inter-related. However, they contain too many permutations in terms of a large group of people – or of any individual for that matter, however typical of that group he might be. Therefore it would not be possible to answer these questions with a reasonable degree of accuracy. To solve this particular problem, the omission approach or implied method is indicated. In other words, while it is essential to identify and analyze the composite parts in order to understand the problem, it is no less essential to realize when that understanding is not a basis for arriving at a solution, but a point of departure towards it.

Having considered the interplay of human emotions involved it will be clear that any attempt at immediate conversion from beer to wine will be unlikely to succeed. However, if one were to concentrate via persuasion to project our inveterate beer drinker as that relatively rare and very special person who feels equally at home with the wine drinking set as with the beer drinking fraternity, one can leave the rest to human nature.

The work illustrated and discussed in this book exemplifies some of the answers to both complex and simple problems, and it is hoped that this introduction will give a better insight into the nature of each problem, together with an understanding of how they were solved, and why a particular method was considered most appropriate or most likely to succeed.

Methods

The classifications under which the examples in this book are discussed are in each case derived principally from the method used. The terms themselves are self-explanatory. It should be noted, however, that many solutions contain at least an element of one or more other methods. More often than not, it is not the actual problem but the idea for its solution which dictates the choice of a particular method.

The criteria for the selection of work were, firstly, the appropriateness of the solution; and, secondly, the quality of each piece of work as a complete entity in itself.

Many advertising agencies have their own yardstick by which the likely success of any campaign is measured. Such a yardstick must inevitably pose a number of questions against which such ideas are tested, and, generally speaking, the idea which answers most or all of these questions is the one adopted. The questions are predictably similar, and are always centred around one fundamental question: what are we trying to say/sell – and to whom?

Much has been made of market research, and large advertising campaigns are, as a rule, based upon their findings and subsequent conclusions. However, such data should always be treated with caution, and it should be remembered that people's stated opinions may not necessarily be true, and even if they are, they are by no means permanent.

Not so long ago, there were many advertising agencies whose chief pride was not their impressive list of clients, but their own creative skill. The fact that the quality of that creative skill was reflected by their list of clients was no mere coincidence. These agencies demanded, encouraged, and sought out the best creative talent, wherever it was to be found. The single-minded men and women who made advertising both exciting and successful by their instinctive understanding of the general public, and their determination to back intuition gained from experience against assembled data, are slowly disappearing.

It is a sad, but hopefully only temporary comment, that the work of agencies and designers is becoming less and less individual, and all too frequently can be distinguished only by the signature – if there is one. But there are successful designers, both old and new, who still persist in following their intuition with creative flair and professional pragmatism. Some of them, famous and unknown, appear in this book.

1. Allegorical

The Ikonolux (1–1) is an advertisement for a range of peak-loading papers of very high quality and precision, manufactured by a German paper mill. Anyone with a knowledge of printing will be well aware of the production problems associated with a peak-loading run. The play on the words 'and it was light' is an extremely fine example of the allegorical approach. This solution, while completely by-passing the technicalities of the subject-matter, nevertheless succeeds admirably in creating an exciting new visual symbol eminently suitable for the purpose.

A company producing a range of *Rainbow* printing inks would want to make the best possible use of its trade name when promoting its products. However, what that company was in this case most interested in was to advertise the fact that its products were particularly good from the point of view of economy, as well as quality. This company has a highly specialized team of expert colour advisers who will forestall or overcome any difficulties encountered in colour printing, and that is how 'the man who brings a rainbow into your life' (1–2) was born.

The client's requirements for the 'Coach tours for everyone' poster (1–3) were to create an image of comfort and relaxation, and to combine with it a clear indication that tours could be arranged to stately homes, palaces, and castles.

In one sense, at least, these two requirements are not compatible. The concepts of comfort and relaxation, when expressed visually, do not go hand in hand with the formal and imposing character of stately homes. But kings are synonymous with palaces and castles, and when they did travel they travelled both in comfort and in coaches.

The sense of history and tradition may be treated in a humorous way, but it is not a matter for irreverent treatment. Although he has no realm to speak of, the playing card king is still a king, and he presented a distinct possibility of combining and conveying both messages without demoting the subject.

The same bus company also runs, and therefore advertises, a regular trip to London, the chief attraction being that London is a conglomeration of famous

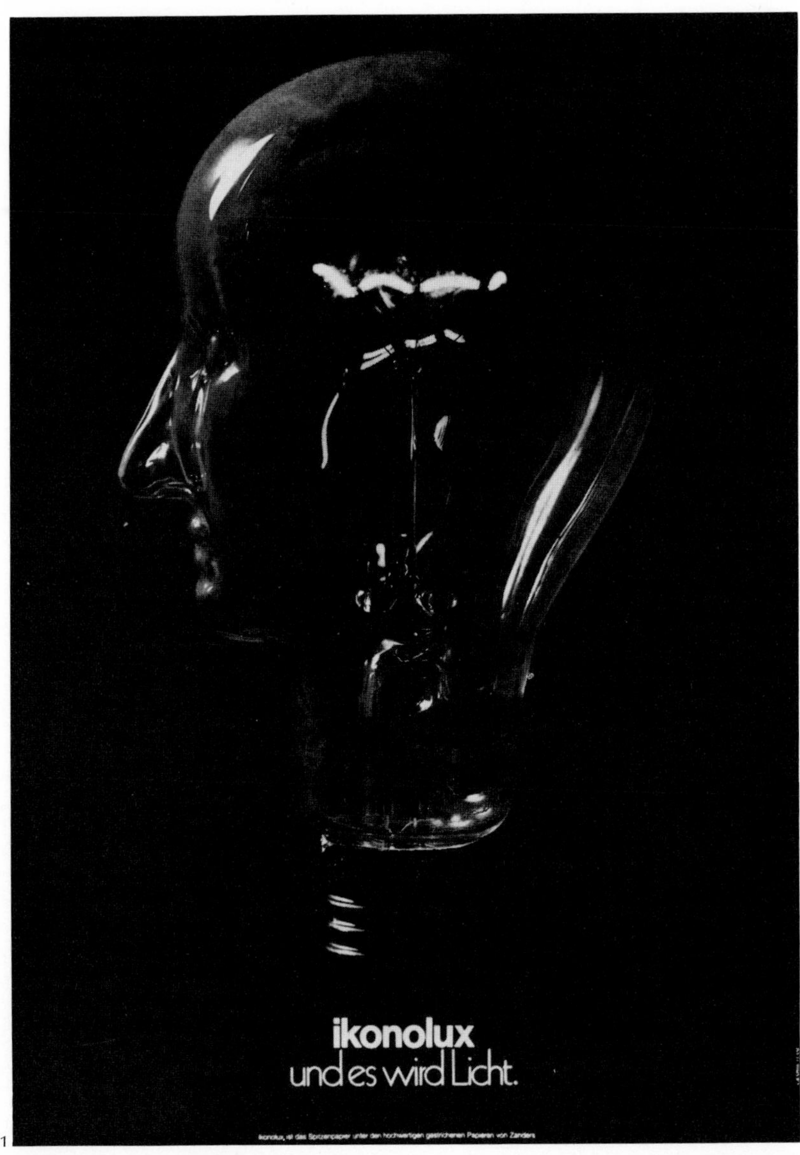
ikonolux
und es wird Licht.
Ikonolux, ist das Spitzenpapier unter den hochwertigen gestrichenen Papieren von Zanders

1-1

landmarks, familiar to people all over the world. It is a city whose face and character are constantly changing. These changes, for the most part, take place unobtrusively, so that only a prolonged lapse of time between one visit and the next makes the difference in scenery or mood particularly noticeable. To the frequent visitor and to the Londoner, the most apparent and notable change in the character of that city is its new and cosmopolitan brightness, and the excitement of its night life. This particular aspect of London was the one to be focused upon.

A new image of London, but with some familiar elements, had to be evolved; and it had to convey the message of brightness and colour without being lurid or sordid – in other words, an allegorical approach was called for (1–4, page 72).

Unlike London, however, most advertisements for a rolling metal door would be factual, technical, or instructive, or possibly all three. After all, there is not a great deal of visual excitement to be elicited from the subject. One lifts up one's arm, and up goes the door – and vice versa.

1-2

Metal doors are normally, but not necessarily always, strong and heavy. They are susceptible to rust, which makes them more difficult to open and shut. This American company makes virtually indestructible, rust-proof metal rolling doors, paying particular attention to the reliability and ease of operating the doors. All these aspects are brilliantly communicated in this example (1–5 – part of advertisement only): Stars and Stripes for the USA; Superman for strength; and flexibility of muscles for ease of operation.

And it is only a door, after all!

Dequadin (1–6) is an 'ethical' medicament for throat infections. ('Ethical', in this context, refers to any form of medicine which is available on prescription only. Palliatives, restoratives, and tablets freely obtainable from pharmacists are called patent medicine.) A direct-mail advertisement was required, which for obvious reasons would be sent to medical practitioners only, and was unlikely ever to be seen by members of the general public.

The specific characteristic and advantage of *Dequadin* is the longer in-and-after action which effectively counteracts the intermittent intensity and variable length of a throat infection. Broadly speaking, a general medical practitioner receives at least one mailing shot every day – thus to attract and retain his or her attention is never an easy task. To synthesize visually the opposing concepts of 'longer lasting' and 'shorter lasting' on one and the same page made that task intrinsically more difficult. Incidentally, note the placing of the word 'infection'.

A situation faced by doctors everywhere is the fact that a patient often arrives at the surgery in a fairly advanced stage of the particular ailment. This usually calls for immediate application of a curative instead of a preventative. More often than not, a full dosage is also required; this creates a problem because high dosages of some medicines produce strong side-effects, and can occasionally even induce another disease. *Colchicine* is used in the treatment of gout. If prescribed early, there will be no side-effects; but if the patient goes late and therefore requires a high dosage, he may experience nausea, vomiting, or diarrhoea.

This advertisement (1–7) is particularly effective in the poignancy and clarity of its message. The caption (not reproduced here): 'You shouldn't have to wait for diarrhoea to get gout relief', speaks for itself.

1-3

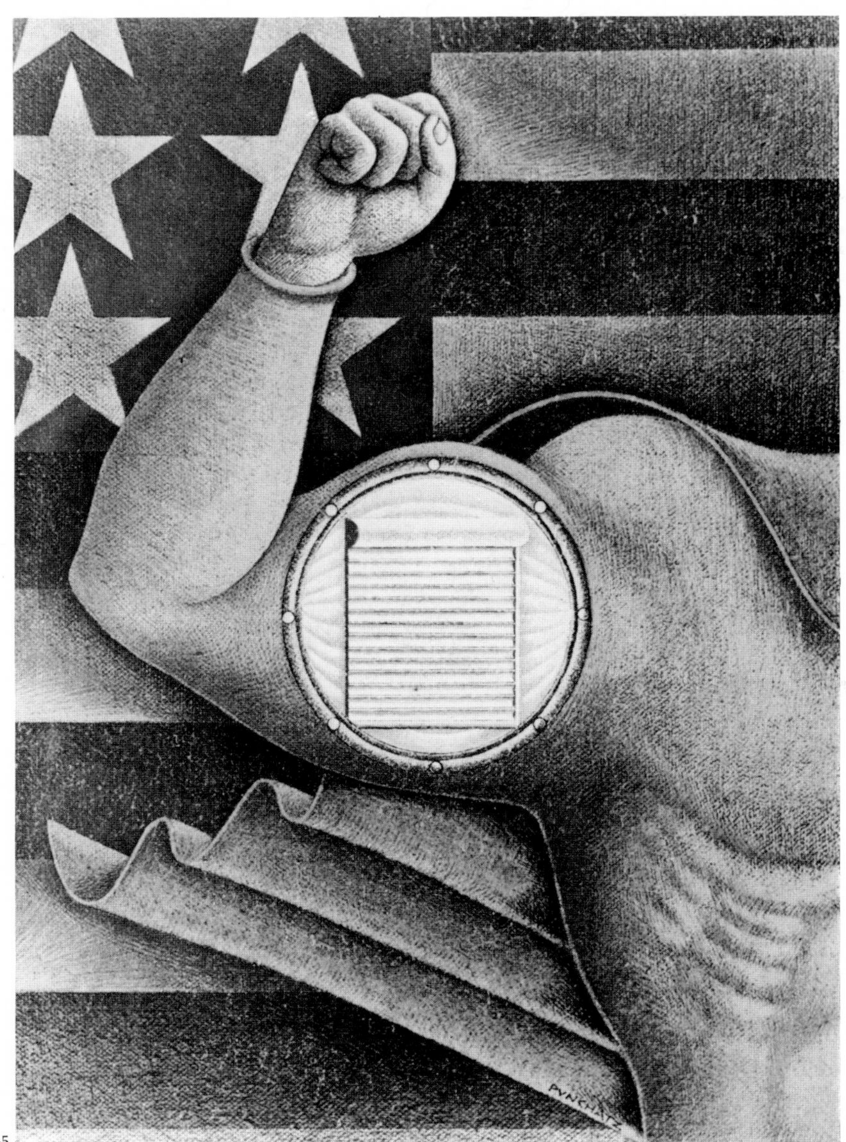

1-5

DEQUADIN
for longer lasting action
and a shorter lasting infection

1-6

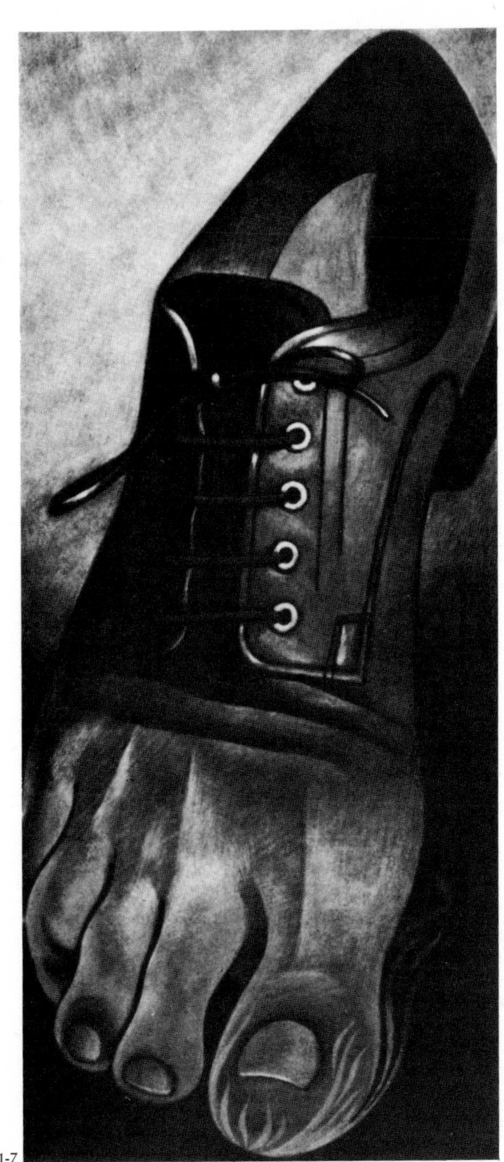

1-7

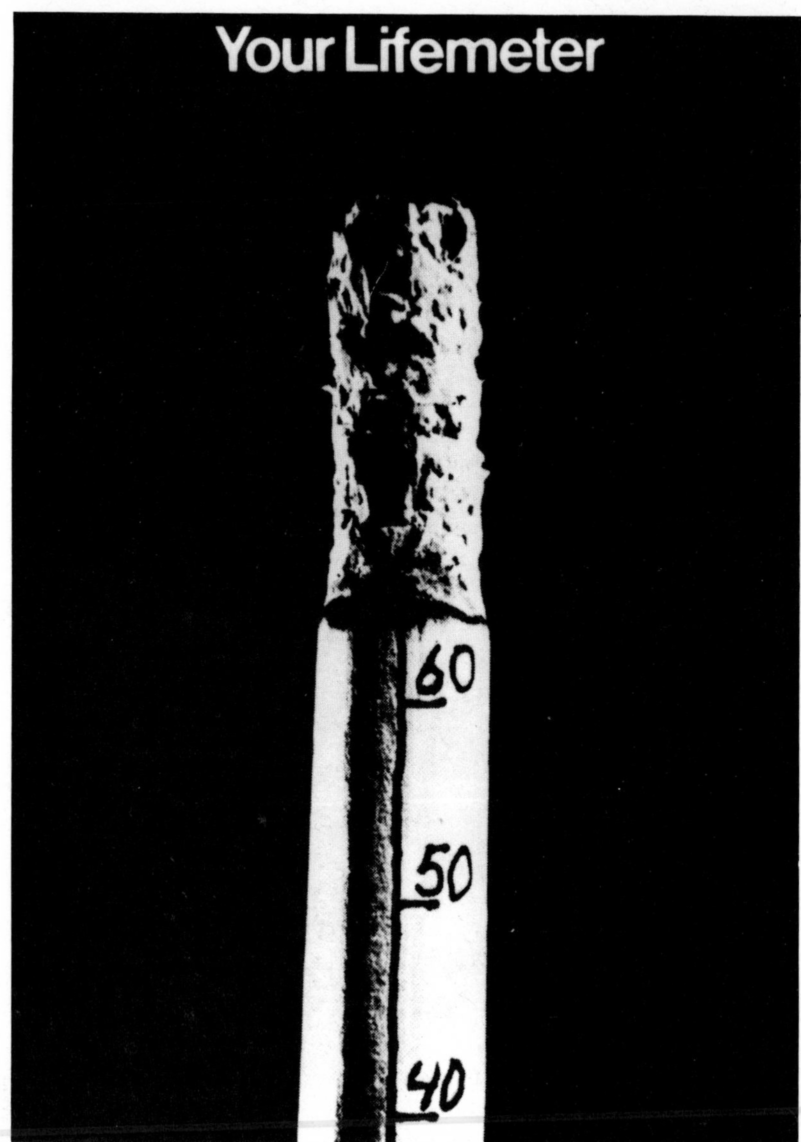

2-1

2. Direct

In the right circumstances, the direct approach can be a most effective means of communication or persuasion because of its straight-to-the-point immediacy. The visual image or language used must be equally simple, uncluttered by superfluous details and devoid of elaboration.

The anti-smoking poster entitled 'Your Lifemeter' (2–1) could hardly be more direct or simple, and the complete lack of adornment considerably strengthens the impact of its message. In no way does it deviate from its intended purpose: to be a cold-blooded warning to us all.

Dequalone is a dermatological ointment. Its curative properties are as important as its protective characteristics, which are five-fold: anti-allergic, anti-bacterial, anti-pruritic, anti-fungal, and anti-inflammatory. Depending on the type and condition of dermatoses, each of these characteristics could assume particular importance. However, to accentuate any one of these characteristics was neither desirable nor indeed possible, because only one advertisement was required by the client. The emphasis was to be on the 'protective' and 'five-fold' elements. Photography or half-tone illustrations could not be used, and simplicity was to be the keyword.

A number of promising possibilities emerged in respect of the 'protective' aspect; but they were soon discarded, as it seemed impossible to integrate the 'five-fold' aspect with any of them. Then a Colt revolver firing five bullets, each one bearing the name of one of the five characteristics, was experimented with at length. This, too, had to be discarded. To give the necessary equal prominence to each characteristic, the bullets had to be the same size, and large enough also to accommodate a fairly long word. The original upright format of the advertisement was not compatible with this. However, the main reason for the increasingly evident lack of conviction and enthusiasm for this idea was the fact that each bullet is fired separately, whereas the protective 'five-fold' action is simultaneous.

One thing leads to another – in this instance a Colt revolver led to a field gun (2–2). The tube of *Dequalone*, which, by the way, had to be included in the advertisement, became the gun barrel.

Having dealt with the ramifications of 'five-fold' protective action, it seems natural to consider another example of the same problem. In the 'triple action cough control' advertisement (2–3), 'triple' is a close relative of 'five-fold', and 'control' is a positive form of protection. The difference between these two solutions is subtle, but important. The first advertisement is concerned with an external ailment, and the second with an internal one. It is no mere coincidence that the three repair men are going *in* while the field gun is firing *outwards*.

Apparently quite oblivious to what is going on around him, the gentleman standing on his head in a bottle of water (2–4) is trying to prove something. He succeeds. 'For a longer lasting breath of fresh air . . .' advertises the effectiveness of a decongestant in naso-pharyngitis and sinusitis. In other words, for someone who until now has suffered from severe nasal congestion, it is a great relief to be able to breathe normally again. And a single administration of *Hazol* nasal drops allows normal breathing to be maintained for up to six hours, because the drops contain a new vasoconstrictor with particularly prolonged action.

To ascertain the precise length of time taken by an activity, or the actual effectiveness of medication, may or may not be relevant. Nevertheless, there are instances when precision of measurements is of paramount importance: for example, in the use of pigments.

Titanium dioxide is a white pigment used extensively in the cosmetics, leather, paint, paper, plastics, and textile industries. It is produced in a variety of types and grades, refined and coarse, according to the particular requirements. Without titanium dioxide pigment as the whitening agent, the bright colours of the products of these industries could not be obtained. The brightness, density, durability, and opacity of the colours are measured by the properties of respective types and grades of pigment, in relation to the material in which they will be used.

The brief was to design a cover for a brochure intended for colour technologists, in which a mass of precise technical data, graphs, and diagrams were set out in tabular form under the general heading 'Colour Measurements'. That heading generated an attempt to translate the concept into a visual idiom, rather than utilize a technical diagram. The directness of the result (2–5, page 72) is created by the visual transliteration of the tape measure into a plausible and pertinent instrument of measure.

A similar degree of visual transliteration is apparent in the 'TRIX . . . . . no moth holes' poster (2–6) for Geigy mothballs. It does not attempt to show the actual moths, either at work or exterminated. Although both are relevant to the problem, neither is in fact relevant to the solution. The moth-eaten glove finger is the result of their presence, and at the same time a very convincing reason for ensuring their future absence.

The final example in this section is a Red Cross poster from Finland (2–7). There is hardly anyone who doesn't know what the red cross symbol stands for, and no one needs reminding what the organization does.

Like the proverbial Good Samaritan, the Red Cross is always compassionate when fellow beings are in distress – regardless of race or religion. But in order to give it is essential to have. What does a Good Samaritan do when he needs help?

2-2

2-6

Geigy
TRIX ... keine Mottenlöcher
HERBERT LEUPIN

2-

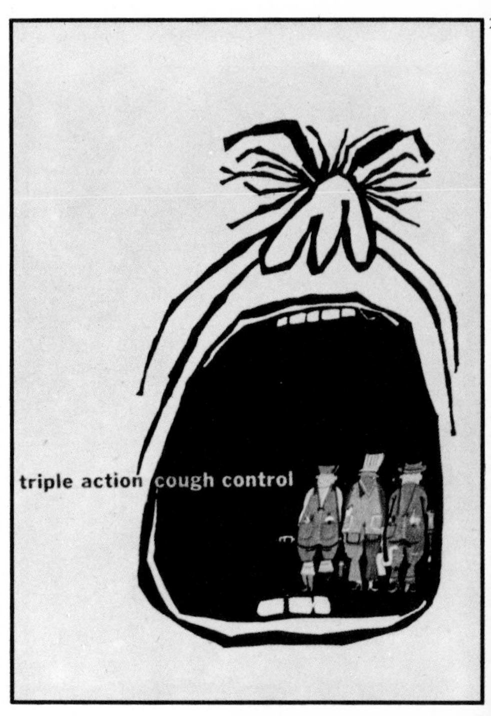
triple action cough control

FOR A LONGER LASTING BREATH OF FRESH AIR..

2-7

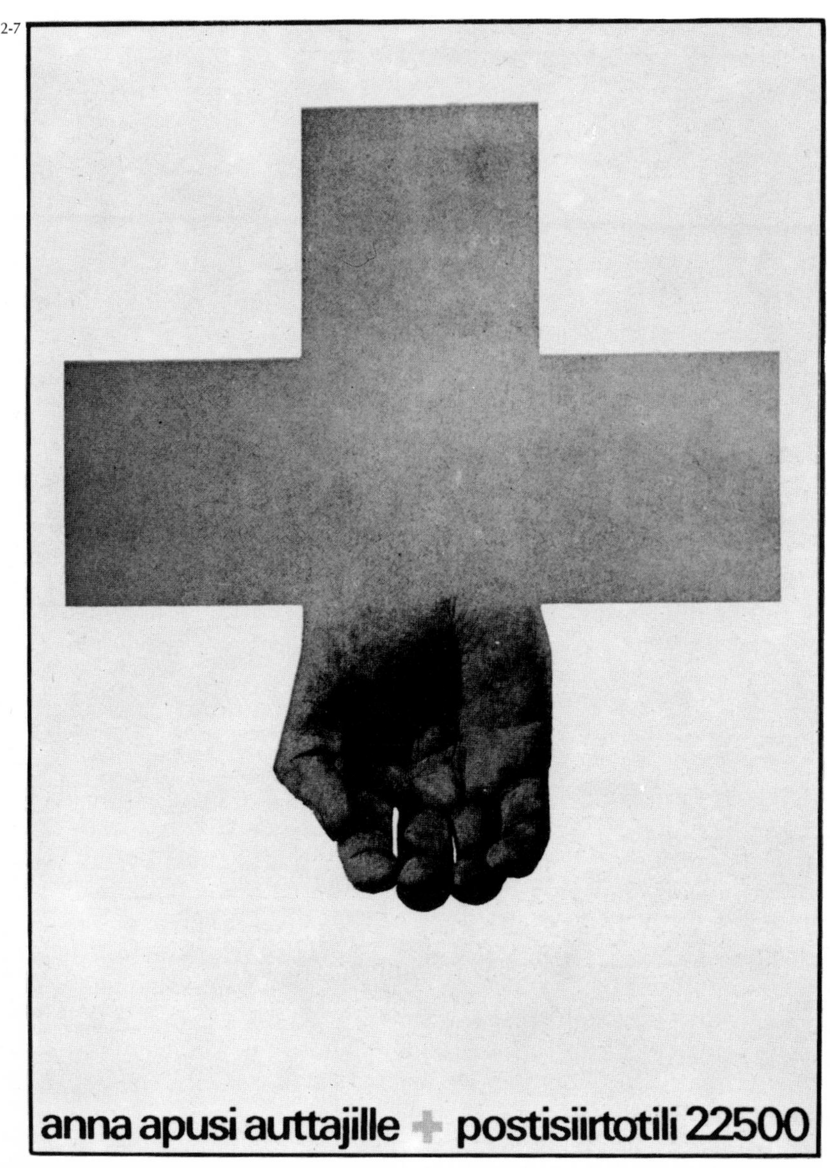
anna apusi auttajille + postisiirtotili 22500

3. Dramatic

The dramatic method is not, strictly speaking, just another form of persuasion. For two specific reasons it is distinctly different from the other methods described here. First, and most important, the dramatic approach is used as the single most effective way of highlighting a serious theme. Second, its use is therefore relatively limited as regards scope and subject. Understandably enough, the power of the dramatic effect results from it being 'too near the truth', and when related to a real issue, or a potentially dangerous situation, it tends to create unease in the audience.

Fictional subjects and ideas are frequently expressed with much greater accent upon the dramatic effect, simply because they *are* fictional, and as such are not directed at anyone specifically.

'Your gossip his guide' by Abram Games (3–1) is the only war poster, as well as the earliest piece of work, appearing in this book. It was not chosen merely to represent the many other excellent war-time posters, nor as a sentimental reminder of times past. It is here because it could not be excluded. The particular brilliance of the idea, its execution, and the sinister effects it creates are really exceptional. True, the fear of submarines is no longer with us. Most likely, too, it has been long forgotten by those who did experience it, and certainly it has no meaning for those who did not.

But if the *impact* of that warning is still so striking today – imagine how powerful it must have been then!

The many aspects of danger, real or imaginary, are continually changing. Regardless of its actual form and nature, a danger axiomatically signifies the presence of some threat, be it from machines, the elements, people, animals, plants, or any combination of these. In each situation, there is the constant common factor of an external threat, except for the real and unpredictable danger which exists within ourselves. But destruction can be caused as much by the application of strength as by its absence to prevent destruction. Thus to 'carry the seeds of one's own destruction', as man is stated to do, is a statement of one's power and strength, and of one's fragility and weakness as well. The consequences of weakness can be singular or manifold. 'Don't blow it with drugs' (3–2) makes it unequivocally clear what the consequences of that particular human weakness are.

3-1

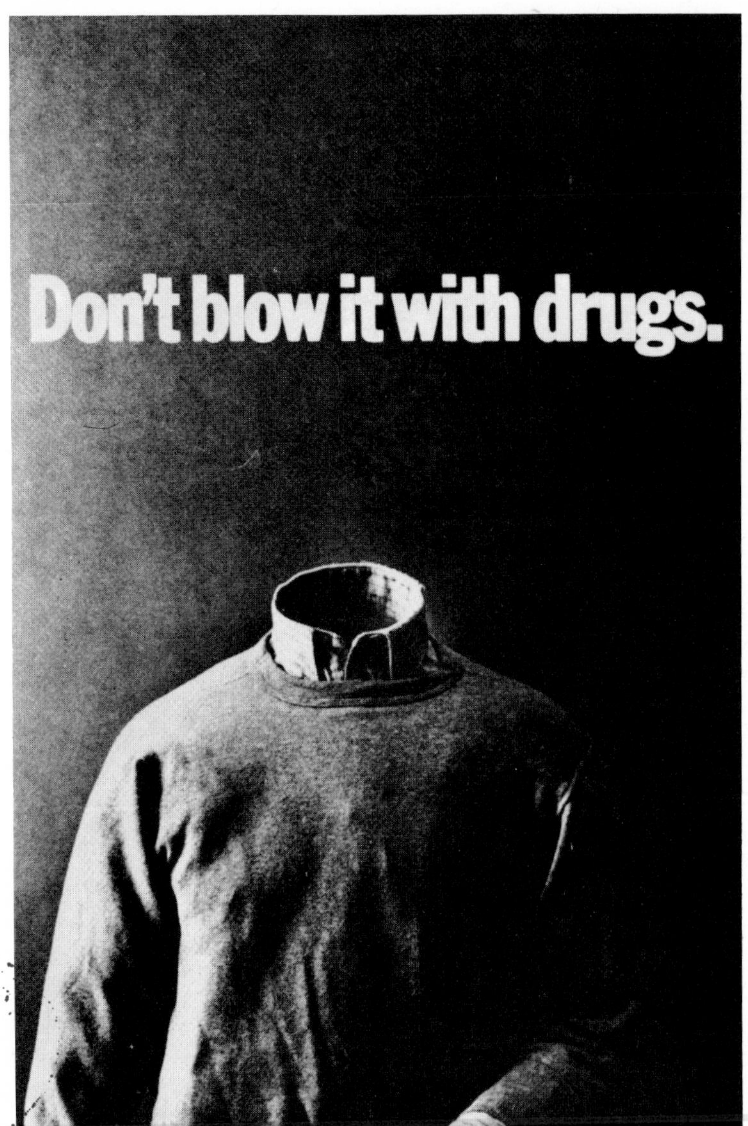

3-2

Whatever the price of weakness or human folly, when that folly is only self-destructive it can be considered the result of a conscious or calculated risk – deliberate choice or imperviousness to reason.

However, choice is not always possible and reason does not necessarily provide a solution. 'Weniger Lärm' (less noise) highlights a problem created by the continually increasing and inescapable volume of noise assailing the human ear and mind (3–3). While it would be perfectly reasonable to suppose that the consequences of noise will not be as dangerous as those of drug addiction, it can also be argued that an assumption can never be used as a substitute for facts, nor as a valid basis for making a positive declaration. But it would be dangerous to wait for facts to become established and for evidence to manifest itself clearly before offering a warning.

The cumulative results of pollution have been apparent for some time, yet despite its recognized threat to life, it goes on seemingly unabated. That much we know already. Whether or not it will eventually destroy the human race, we do not know. Whether the last few survivors really would look like the Cyclopean apparition in 'Zoom contre la pollution de l'oeil' (3–4) is not the point. That image of mutilation is neither misleading nor prophetic, but a glimpse at the awful possibilities inherent in the 'seeds of one's own destruction'.

The pessimist, if asked, might define the difference between reality and fiction as the difference between today and tomorrow. The optimist would no doubt point out, with some pride and a great deal of truth, that many facts of today are the offspring of yesterday's fiction. There are also many facts which are not directly related to one's personal experience. The lack of tactile sensation or emotional involvement reduces them to the level of a fictional reality.

The two film posters – for *Cena Strachu* ('The Price of Fear') from Poland (3–5), and *Anatomy of a Murder* from the USA (3–6) – and the British record sleeve for Berlioz's *Symphonie fantastique* (3–7, page 72), are all examples of fictional reality. It is interesting to note that, although from geographically distant places, they have much in common in their treatment of the subject-matter. All three are analytically resolved, and each one is visually condensed in order to achieve maximum impact, and dramatic effect focused upon its theme. The price of fear is frightening, and, as befits anatomy, the murder is cold and clinical. The nightmarish mixture of death and unattainable love is a chilling spectre.

All the above subjects are serious, and all serious subjects generate their own sense of drama. The personal or emotional involvement, when present, is as capable of converting fiction into fact as it is of distorting fact through the imagination. Perhaps it is often only a predilection for the dramatic which produces personal involvement in a serious subject. The truth may, indeed, be stranger than fiction.

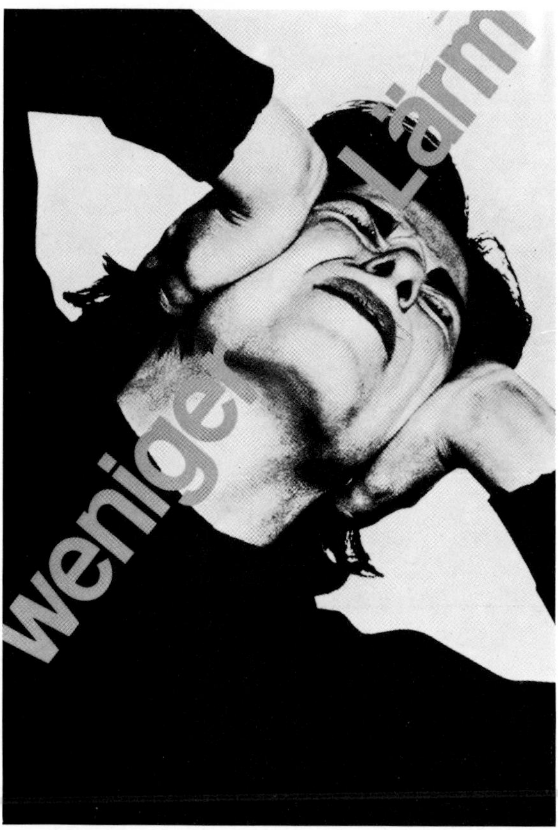

3-3

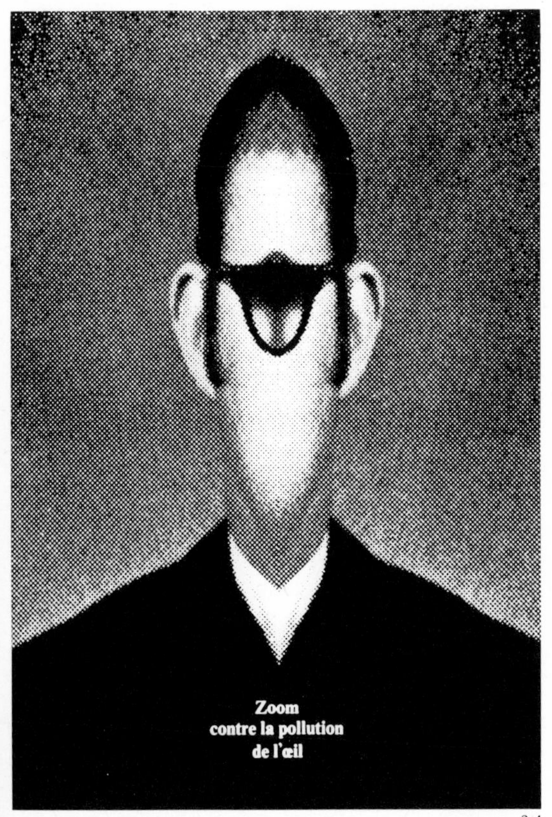
Zoom
contre la pollution
de l'œil

3-4

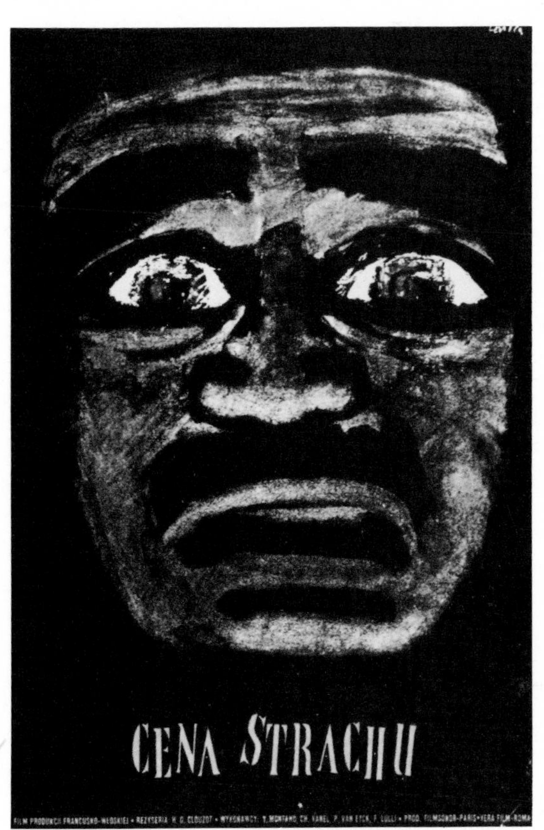
CENA STRACHU

3-5

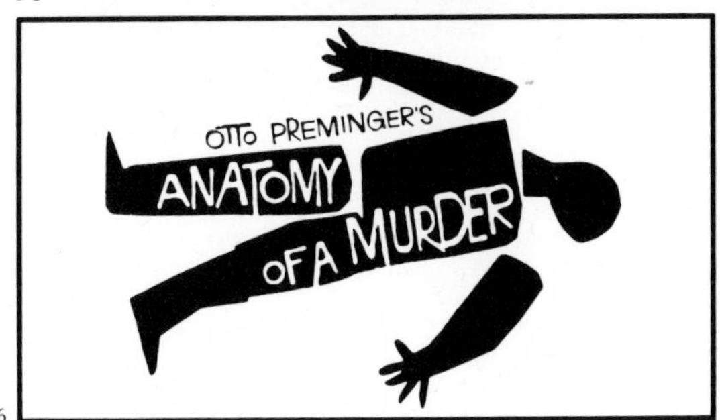
OTTO PREMINGER'S
ANATOMY
OF A MURDER

3-6

4. Emotive

Emotions, while perfectly possible to control for however long it might be desirable or necessary, are impossible to ignore, let alone eradicate. Self-centred or altruistic, self-motivated or aroused by other people, they govern our actions and rule our lives. Without emotions there would be neither love nor war. Voltaire once said: 'To people who think, life is a comedy; and to those who feel, it's a tragedy'. Perhaps so, but in presupposing such a clear-cut division it seems more an attempt to define comedy and tragedy than thinking and feeling. In terms of human emotions it seems inconceivable that feeling and thinking can be divorced from each other. Indeed, it could be argued that without thinking there can be no feeling; that each can only result from and reflect the depth of the other. However, one is also tempted to suggest that tragedy can result from thinking – thinking too much about oneself, and consequently thinking too little about others.

Whether empathy creates sympathy, or sympathy creates empathy, is a debatable question. But there is no doubt that persuasion is only possible in the presence of an emotion – be it overt or subliminal. Thus the aims of persuasion are to render the subconscious conscious; to make a half-felt intention a positive action. 'Call your mother. She worries' (4–1) has very powerful emotive connotations. Playing on a guilt complex arising from neglect, indifference, laziness, or failing in one's filial duty, it succeeds in activating a positive response. The footnote promises instant fulfilment of filial duty with the minimum of effort ('faster than writing'), and at minimum cost ('cheaper than travelling'). 'Easier than yelling' implies that getting in touch with your mother right now will prevent a difficult situation later.

Even if this is no more than an inapplicable emotional reminder, the chances are that you will end up phoning an old or long-forgotten friend. Which is exactly what the telephone company wants you to do – use the phone, and frequently.

Call your mother. She worries.

Calling is faster than writing. Cheaper than traveling. And easier than yelling.

AT&T
and Associated Companies

4-1

Tension is perhaps best described as a halfway house between an emotion and its consequences. Even if that emotion is escalated out of all proportion, and the consequences exist only in the imagination, as they often do, it will be real enough to the person concerned, and sufficient to obscure the sense of judgement or cause a hasty decision.

The crumbling heart on the cover design for 'The roots of marital tension' (4–2) conveys most effectively the essence of one emotional conflict and its consequences. Because of its non-specific and symbolic simplicity, it is equally pertinent to any of the causes of marital tension. The heart symbol conveys the impression of 'the bottom dropping out of the marriage', but at the same time it is quite clear that the pieces *can* be fitted together again.

Far more serious, though, is that state of emotional conflict which, alone or combined with other factors, induces suicidal tendencies. It is not very clear why suicide, however real and tragic, still remains a subject of social and religious taboo. Whatever the moral implications may be, the fact remains that suicide, attempted or committed, is an act of self-destruction. The majority of suicides are probably a direct or indirect result of unacceptable social values or the uninhabitable environment. In either situation, suicide is an escape from a reality with which the individual could not or did not want to cope.

However, it would be very misleading to create the impression that society and the medical profession neither want to know nor care. On the contrary, they both know and care very much. These comments are made partly as general background, and partly to point out the complex network of external factors over and above the inherent difficulties facing any designer involved with the subject of suicide as a problem in visual communication.

The Geigy Company produced and donated this cover design (4–3) for a brochure written and issued by the Center for Studies of Suicide Prevention, and it is an excellent solution to such a problem.

For many people, however, the will to live transcends all suffering and imaginable misfortune. This will to live makes them rationalize emotion and experience, because to survive it is necessary to understand. But the knowledge of not being wanted – of being a 'displaced person' – must be, surely, the most shattering experience, and the least comprehensible. The expression of those trapped-in, pleading, disbelieving eyes, staring from behind the prison-like bars of the elongated letters 'D' and 'P', is an eloquent visual monument to such an experience (4–4).

The Stars and Stripes painted on the face of a coloured American, appealing for 'liberty and justice for all' (4–5), is another solution to a similar problem.

It has already been mentioned that it is often the proffered solution to the problem which dictates the choice of a particular method, and the 'Don't take chances!' poster for industrial safety (4–6) exemplifies this point particularly well. The contrast between treatment and subject is striking, but the humorous approach enhances rather than diminishes the seriousness of the subject and the consequences of ignoring the warning.

The roots
of marital tension

Patterns of Tension No. 6

4-2

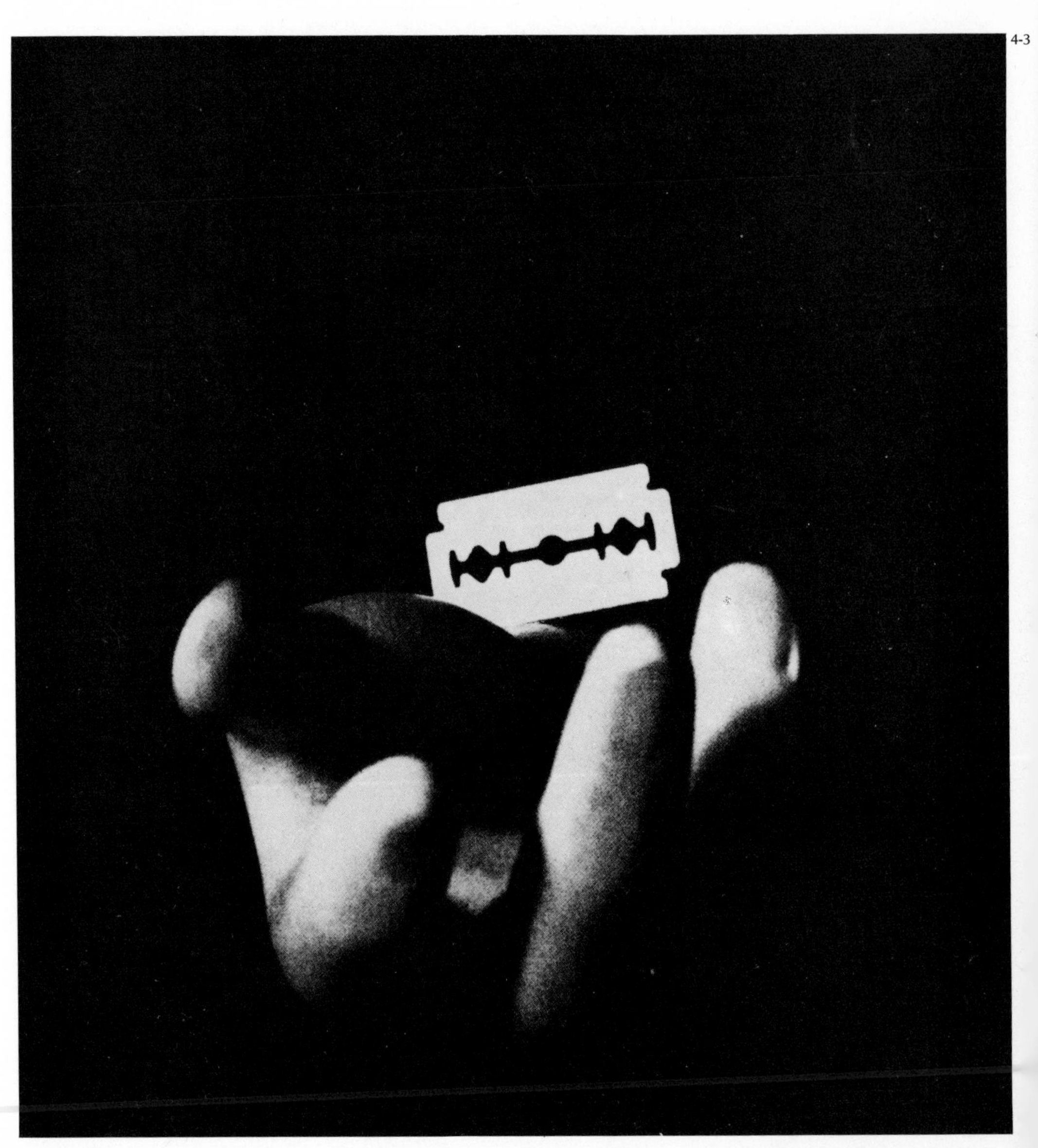

4-3

Emotions, however, are not always a reflection of the dangers inherent in daily life, or an expression of feelings arising from interaction between two or more people. Our personal appearance also exerts a considerable influence on the way we feel, and correspondingly affects our reactions to the world around us. Whether a hair-do or a new dress make a girl feel better because she looks more attractive, or vice versa, is not really relevant. The fact is that for a while she *does* feel superior, or more self-assured and confident, at least. The press advertisement for the Steiner Salon in London (4–7) was designed to capitalize on that feeling, and at the same time to stress that an appointment was essential. The copy 'Superiority complex by appointment and the hair style to match' sums it up in a point-blank message.

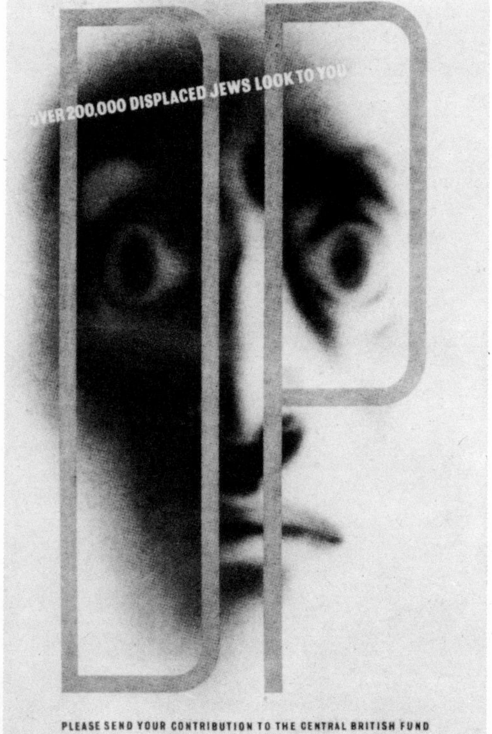

DP
OVER 200,000 DISPLACED JEWS LOOK TO YOU
PLEASE SEND YOUR CONTRIBUTION TO THE CENTRAL BRITISH FUND

4-4

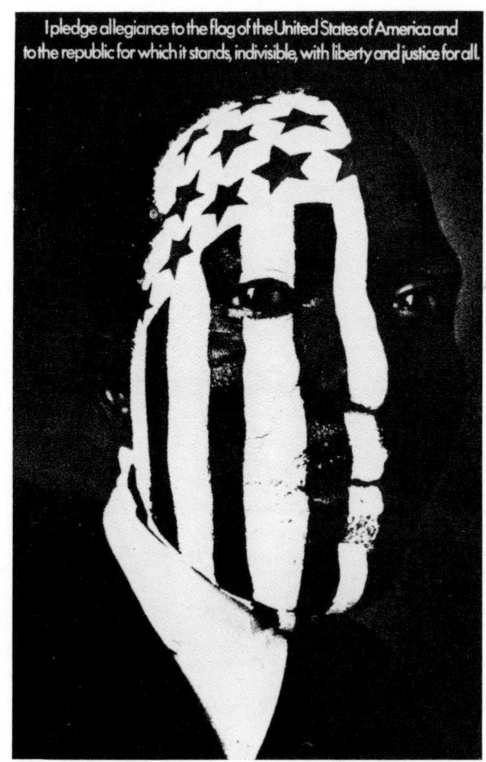

I pledge allegiance to the flag of the United States of America and to the republic for which it stands, indivisible, with liberty and justice for all.

4-5

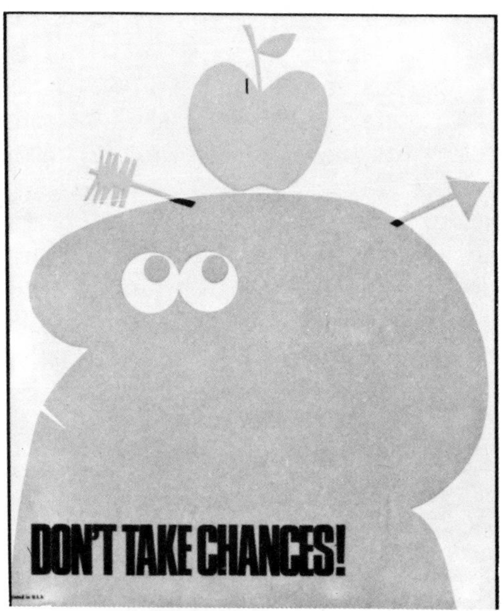
DON'T TAKE CHANCES!

4-6
4-7

SUPERIORITY
COMPLEX BY
APPOINTMENT
AND
THE HAIR STYLE
TO MATCH

5. Illustrative

The spectrum of visual appeal that can be generated by the illustrative method is both wide and varied. Be it alluring, poignant, chilling, educating, mouth-watering, or simply revealing, this method can be a very potent and highly effective means of persuasion.

As a method in itself, it does differ significantly and in many respects from all the other methods discussed in this book. To begin with, its application unquestionably requires more skill and sensitivity, because the margin of error is very small indeed. Usually the method either works in absolute terms, or it does not work at all. For obvious reasons, it is in most cases unlikely to achieve the desired effect or create the expected response without the use of colour: to give an obvious example, there is a world of difference between a monochrome and a colour photograph of a glass of beer or a bowl of cherries.

According to particular requirements, the illustrative method is primarily used as an action-stimulant or as a preventive-motivator. Broadly speaking, the method falls into two distinct categories, each serving a specific purpose. The first aims to accentuate the factual realism, and the second to stimulate fictional reality. This may seem a contradiction in terms, but factual realism exists simultaneously in fact and in one's experience, whereas fictional reality only exists in fact but not in one's experience (sometimes, of course, as for instance in the realm of fantasy or science fiction, it may not exist in either). In other words, one's personal experience of pain becomes the factual reality of pain, while to another person who knows of its existence but has never suffered from it, it will remain as a fiction of reality only.

If truth *is* stranger, or more potent, than fiction, it is not altogether surprising that the illustrative method invariably has to underplay the reality of socially sensitive and morally controversial subjects. When thought necessary, its potency is deliberately muted by diffusing the effectiveness of its clarity and visual impact. However, it might also be suggested that a protest voiced against an 'objectionable' or 'offensive' photograph or design is not necessarily motivated by a self-professed concern for the feelings of others, but more by an uneasy conscience or the stirring of some dormant, unwelcome memory. Advertising, however unwittingly, can and does produce social side-effects, which in the mind of the moralist constitute a convincing, if misplaced, argument against it. Taking the excellent 'cherry pie tin' photograph (5–1, page 68) by Don Last as an example, the accentuation of reality is so compelling that the moralist could postulate a very plausible argument against it as being anti-social because it will make fat people fatter, and will not help those too poor to eat.

To deny the existence of such people would be the height of irresponsibility in both human and professional terms. There are several answers which could solve the *real* problem, but since the moralist's concern here is confined solely to side-effects, one may be forgiven for suggesting that to ban the manufacture and sale of cherry pies is, of course, the most obvious remedy!

The examples here represents a wide cross-section of the use of the illustrative method, and are worth close study if only to show why they have succeeded, and to indicate how much more can still be achieved.

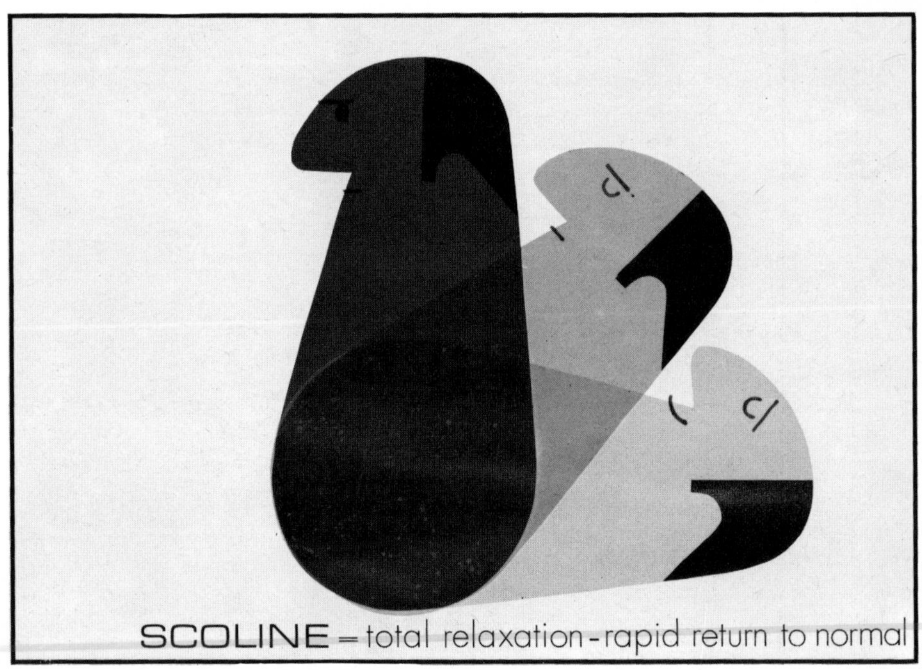
SCOLINE = total relaxation - rapid return to normal

5-2

5-3

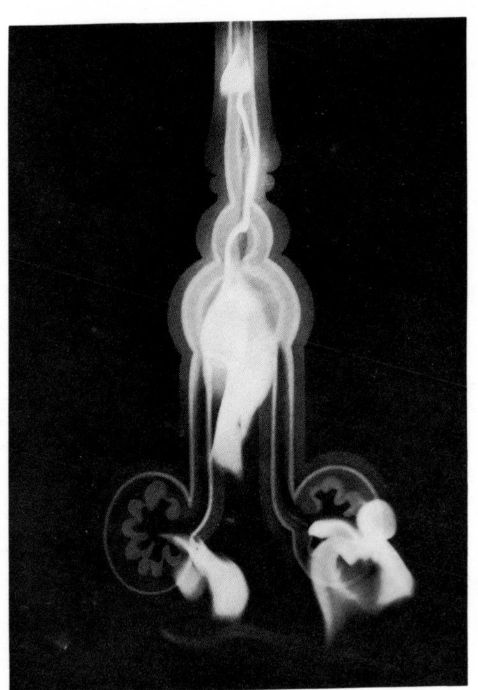

5-4

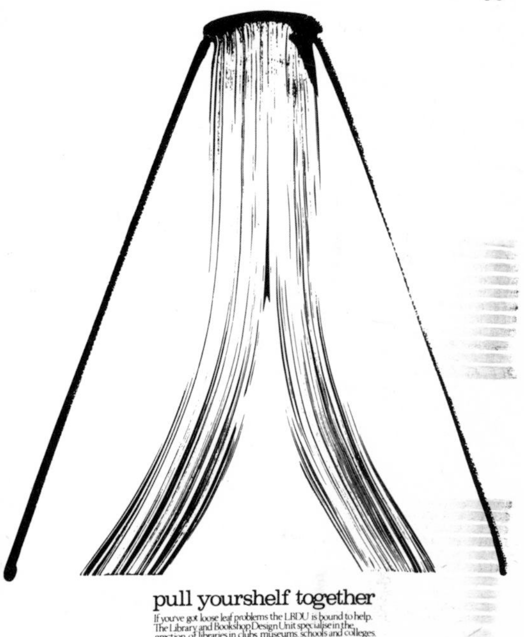
pull yourshelf together
If you've got loose leaf problems the LBDU is bound to help.
The Library and Bookshop Design Unit specialise in the
erection of libraries in clubs, museums, schools and colleges.
Make your appointment now, or just book in advance.

5-5

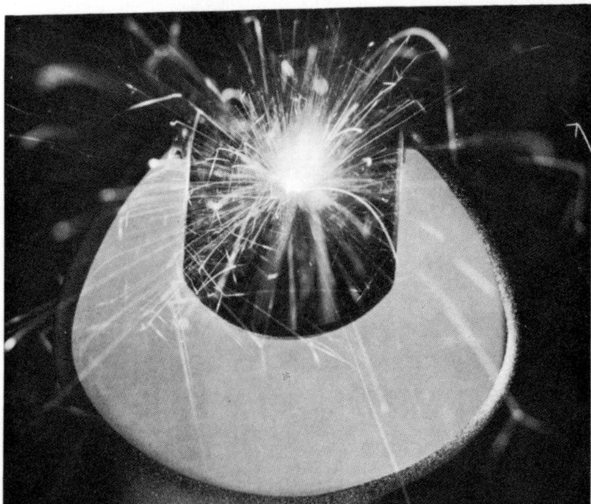

5-6

5-7

6-3

karo
whatever the rhinovirus CAPRITON controls the symptoms

6. Impact

Impact is created entirely by the element of the unexpected, and the greater that element of the unexpected, the harder will be the impact. The inherent element of surprise is obviously the chief catalyst, but anticipating a number of possible outcomes in any given situation does not, in any way, preclude the element of surprise. What it does do is to confine that element within the bounds of *expected* possibilities, thus maintaining feasibility in relation to one's imagination and past experience. Whatever the final outcome, the scale of registered surprise will be correspondingly reduced according to the degree of anticipation.

As the word implies, the unexpected is not tangible, and as such it cannot be factually considered, or calculated. Therein lies its real power of impact, and ability to shock. Often enough the cause of the impact is so disproportionate to its effect that it can magnify the latter beyond the point of coherence, and in extreme cases beyond the point of no return.

As an aspect of visual communication, the impact method is not as frequently used as might be thought. Its application is somewhat limited, and in practice confined to a strong surprise rather than a mild shock treatment. It appears in pharmaceutical and ethical medicine advertising more than in other areas, because such advertising is aimed at the medical profession only and is therefore seldom, if ever, seen by the general public. Most important of all, it is concerned with the realities of life and death, which produce their own inimitable shock value. But even here the application is muted, and the actual impact is wrapped in the cotton wool of implied rather than direct delivery.

The impact method is also eminently suitable in situations where a particular aspect of a problem or a solution needs to be very heavily emphasized. Such over-emphasis can be achieved, as will be seen in the accompanying illustrations, by the use of close-up, contrast, isolation, magnification and, last but not least, the unexpected.

The Roche advertisement 'Romilar – real progress in fighting coughs' (6–1) is a good example of the close-up genre. It was designed as a full page colour-spread. The over-emphasis of the abnormally red face demonstrates very convincingly the effect of a persistent and chronic cough. There are no unnecessary details to dilute its striking impact, and no elaboration of the image to obscure its message.

The poster for the Stuttgart Zoo (6–2), designed by Hans Lohrer, uses the symbol of the zoo as the pupil of the zebra's eye. It has no wording – itself a rare achievement. The animal looks very alive, notwithstanding the simplicity of its form verging on abstraction.

The rhinovirus (6–3) is real enough, but it is not to be found either in the tropics or in the zoo. For reasons better known to the bacteriologists working in the Salisbury Colds Research Centre, it happens to live in one's nostrils at least some of the time. The rhinovirus hails from a rather large family of about thirty varieties of common cold virus. One tiny capsule of *Capriton* keeps them at bay, or ensures their speedy departure if already present. This example was designed as one of a series of three double-page advertisements, to appear in medical journals. The only colour used was red for the caption 'whatever the rhinovirus CAPRITON controls the symptoms'. It relies partly on the impact created by disproportionate emphasis, and partly on being provided with a ready-made symbol from the subject matter.

'Vite Aspro', a poster by Savignac (6–4), combines nearly all the ingredients of the impact method, with over-emphasis on the suffering and volume of an unbearable headache. The word 'vite', meaning quick, can be interpreted here both as a cry for help, and as a statement of the speed of the medicament in question. The roar of ceaseless heavy traffic permeated with the cacophony of klaxons is well known to the inhabitants of large towns, in France or anywhere else. As it happens, the poster was not apparently to everybody's liking, and was considered somewhat cruel. Too effective might perhaps be a more appropriate description.

The power of impact, modified or raw, has a language of its own. Essentially it is a language of simplicity. To be effective, and it can be devastatingly so, it demands a finely tuned balance between the acceptable and the unexpected, with a predilection for adventure into unexplored regions. For these reasons alone it is, perhaps, the most difficult to learn and the most exciting to master.

Romilar
ROCHE
wirklicher Fortschritt in der Hustenbekämpfung

6-1

vite
'ASPRO'

6-4

6-2

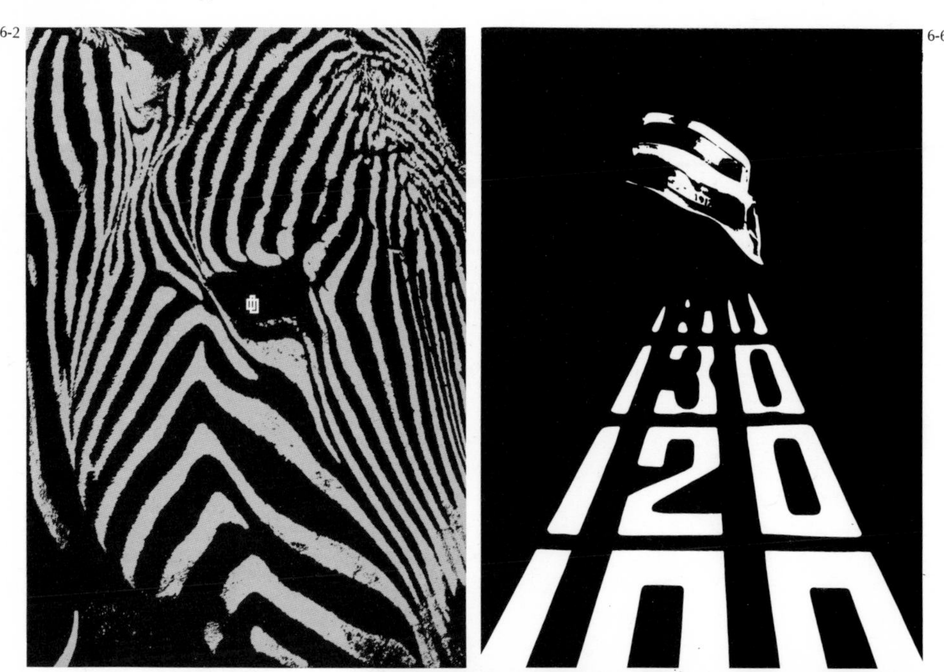

6-6

Wenn der Wurm drin ist
Molevac
Das neue 1-Dosis-Oxyuricid ist einfach: Eine einmalige Dosis genügt, um die Madenwurminfektionen in nahezu allen Fallen sicher zu beseitigen. Die orale Vertraglichkeit ist ausgezeichnet. Nebenwirkungen allgemeiner Art sind nicht zu befurchten, da Molevac nicht resorbiert wird.
Dosierung: 1 Teeloffel Molevac Suspension pro 10 kg Korpergewicht.
Kleinkinderpackung: Flasche mit 10 ccm
Originalpackung: Flasche mit 25 ccm
Familienpackung: Flasche mit 75 ccm
Parke Davis, Munchen

6-5

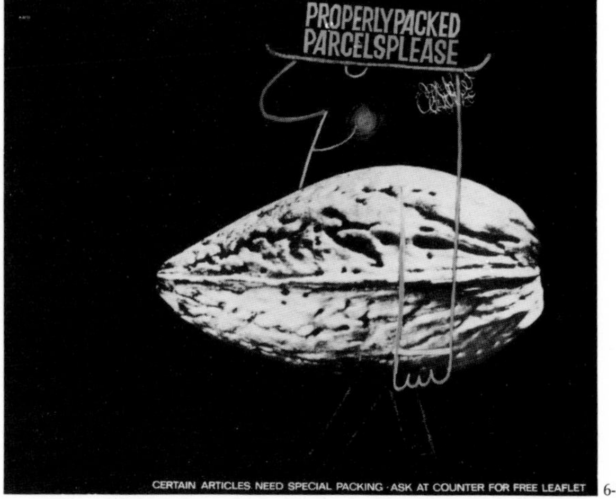
PROPERLYPACKED
PARCELSPLEASE
CERTAIN ARTICLES NEED SPECIAL PACKING · ASK AT COUNTER FOR FREE LEAFLET

6-7

7. Implied

The popular opinion in the Western hemisphere, that a man must be effeminate unless he exudes the smell of a pipe, stale cigarettes, leather, or some other, but never clearly specified, 'masculine' tang, is largely a thing of the past, although still alive in some quarters. The use of an after-shave toilet preparation, formerly the prerogative of the eccentric few, has now become commonplace, and is no longer a cause for raised eyebrows. People concerned with advertising after-shave toiletries are well aware that the creation of a new image of the 'scented man' is essential. Many advertisements have been designed with obvious male overtones, and such brand names as *Brut*, *Karate*, and *Tabac* are a case in point.

'Why don't you take the 8-45 instead?' (7–1) is an advertisement for the *King's Men* range of after-shave toilet preparations, which renders further comment utterly superfluous.

But if the implications of '. . . take the 8-45 instead' are easy to imagine, what is the image of the imagination itself, and how can it be visualized in a tangible form understood by everyone? Opinions will differ, as will the solutions, but they all depend on one's perception of visual experience and ability to perceive. The power of recall, be it instant or total, is often mistakenly described as imagination, whereas in fact the real imagination is a faculty of the intellect. 'Imagine what you could do . . . if you could do everything you imagine' (7–2, page 61) is a booklet cover illustration which is the result of such an imagination.

The fact that we use superlatives so readily and frequently diminishes their value as linguistic currency to the point of being taken as a sweeping statement, rather than being accepted as an expression of real or relative truth. In advertising, the use of superlatives is by no means motivated only by a desire to *appear* better – it is often the right language to describe something which really *is* better. But 'better' can also be inadequate, and 'new' need not mean different. However, what does one say about a product which really *is* better, different, and new? And how does one say it?

The product is a chair, hand-made throughout, constructed from a top-quality material, and subjected to rigorous tests by Harvey Probber Inc., the manufacturers. The answer (7–3) is as simple as it is unexpected: 'If your Harvey Probber chair wobbles, straighten your floor'.

The *Ty-phoo* tea advertisement (7–4) is shown here as a good and carefully considered example of the implied method; note that it is also devoid of superlatives.

Advertisements for new, popular, special, or seasonal books, as well as for numerous book clubs, are a permanent feature of many magazines and newspapers. Each book presents a distinct opportunity, if not a necessity, for a different approach or visual interpretation. A library, however, has all kinds of books, catering for the whole spectrum of interests from science fiction at one end to works of reference at the other. To encompass such a vast range of subjects in one visual idiom is far from easy. To create and express an image of the library as a treasure-house of knowledge, experience, and emotion is infinitely more difficult.

The 'abcdefghijklmnopqrstuvwxyz – your public library has these arranged in ways that make you cry, giggle, love, hate, wonder, ponder and understand' poster (7–5) is for a National Library Week, sponsored by the National Book Committee Inc. in co-operation with the American Library Association. It was awarded a medal by the Art Directors' Club of New York.

Books are for reading, but lipstick (7–6) is for lips – and lips are for passing information. Their shape and the colour of the lipstick alone could tell what the lady has in mind, how she feels, and what mood she is in, or wants to be in. Each colour conveys a separate and distinctly different message. Often enough that message will no longer be valid by the time it reaches the eyes of the intended recipient. Yet it does not lose its point, because it will tell him about the original intentions of the lady. Sometimes, of course, it is still there only to make him realize what the real intention might have been. A veritable armoury of instant communication 'for every possible occasion' – and real enough ammunition on the lips of an expert.

The mood of carefree gaiety portrayed by a harlequin character blowing a paper raspberry (7–7) suggests a good party. Of course, no-one deliberately goes to a party to be miserable or for the explicit purpose of refusing another drink, by saying: 'No thank you, I'm driving', or, worse still, to restrain someone else because he is driving. Everybody wants to have a good time and know he will still get back home safely– and the coach driver will make sure of it. The play on the double meaning of the word 'party' has extended the range of implications.

7-4

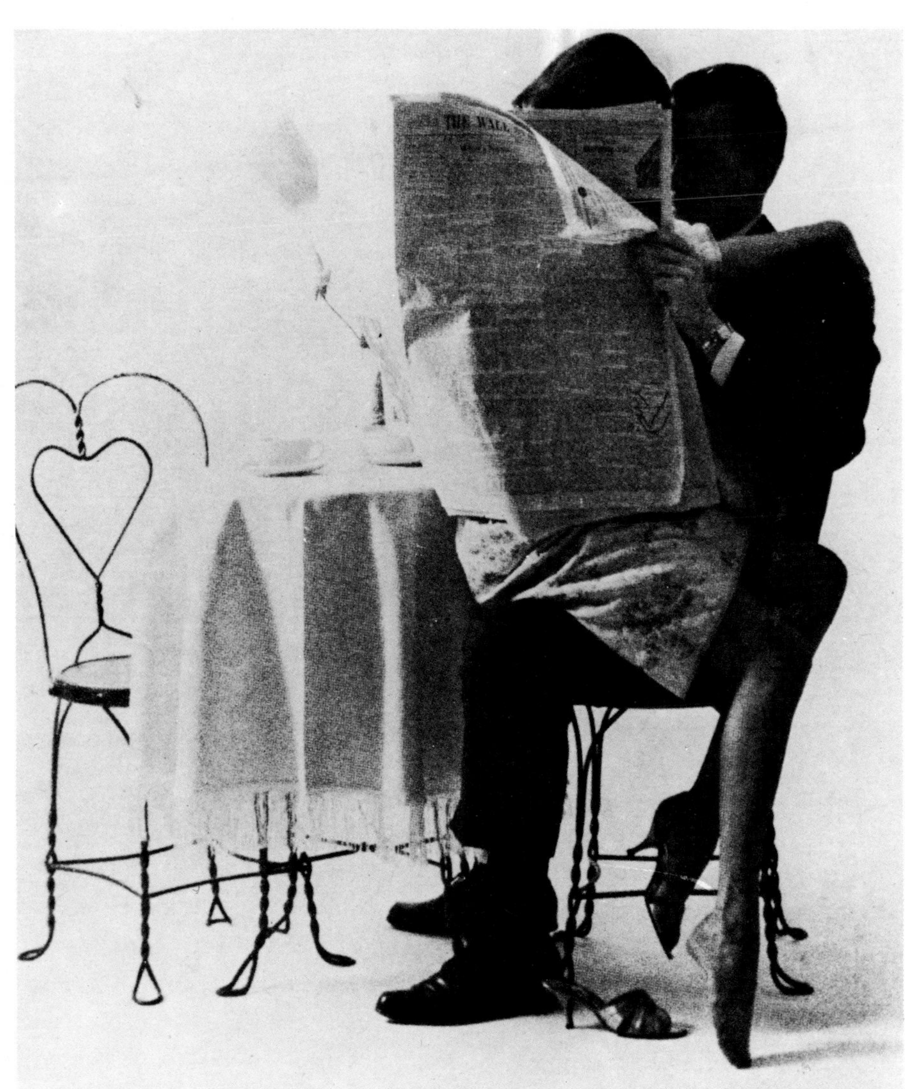
"Why don't you take the 8:45 instead?"

7-1

7-6

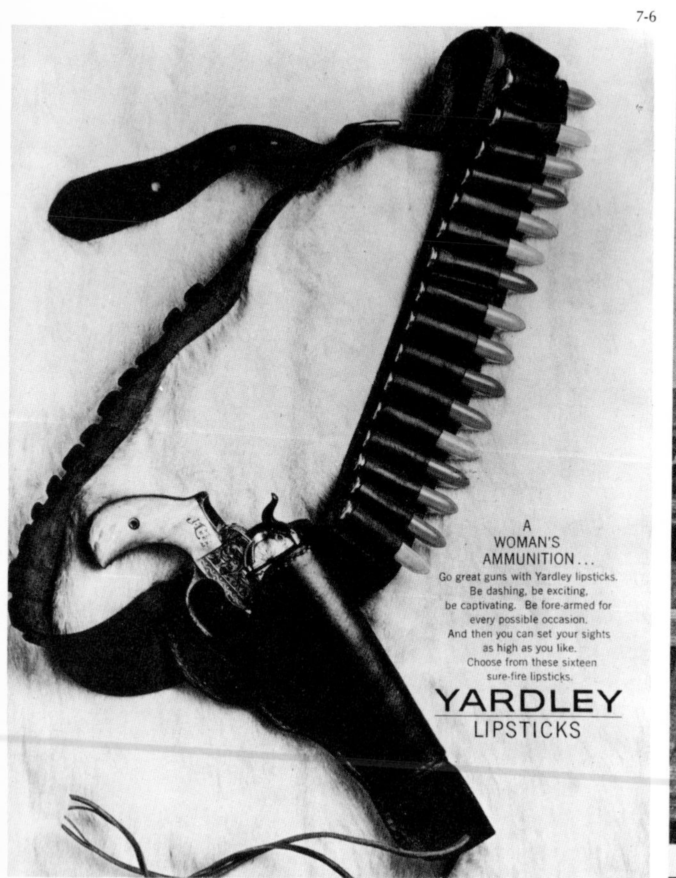
A
WOMAN'S
AMMUNITION . . .
Go great guns with Yardley lipsticks.
Be dashing, be exciting,
be captivating. Be fore-armed for
every possible occasion.
And then you can set your sights
as high as you like.
Choose from these sixteen
sure-fire lipsticks.
YARDLEY
LIPSTICKS

7-3

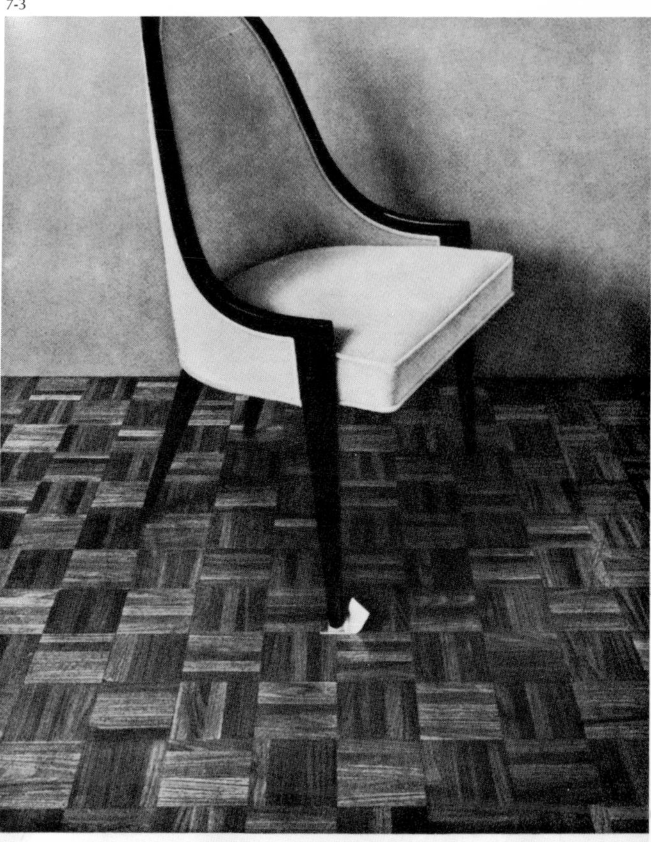
If your Harvey Probber chair wobbles, straighten your floor.

7-5

abcdefghijklmnopqrstuvwxyz

Your public library has these arranged in ways that make you cry, giggle, love, hate, wonder, ponder and understand.

It's astonishing what those twenty-six little marks can do.

In Shakespeare's hands they became *Hamlet*.

Mark Twain wound them into *Huckleberry Finn*. James Joyce twisted them into *Ulysses*. Gibbon pounded them into *The Decline and Fall of the Roman Empire*. Milton shaped them into *Paradise Lost*. Einstein added some numbers and signs (to save time and space) and they formed *The General Theory of Relativity*.

Your name is in them.

And here we are, using them now.

Why? Because it's National Library Week—an excellent time to remind you of letters, words, sentences and paragraphs. In short, *books—reading*.

You can live without books, of course. But it's so *limiting*.

How else can you go to Ancient Rome? Or Gethsemane? Or Gettysburg?

Or meet such people as Aristotle, F. Scott Fitzgerald, St. Paul, Byron, Napoleon, Genghis Khan, Tolstoi, Thurber, Whitman, Emily Dickinson and Margaret Mead?

To say nothing of Gulliver, Scarlett O'Hara, Jane Eyre, Gatsby, Oliver Twist, Heathcliffe, Captain Ahab, Raskolnikov and Tom Swift.

With books you climb Everest, drop to the bottom of the Atlantic. You step upon the Galapagos, sail alone around the world, visit the Amazon, the Antarctic, the Nile.

You can learn how to do anything from cooking to repairing a television set.

With books you can explore the past, guess at the future and make sense out of today.

Read. Your public library has thousands of books, all of which are yours for the asking.

And add books to your *own* library. With each book you add, your home grows bigger and more interesting.

National Library Week, April 16-22—sponsored by the National Book Committee, Inc., in cooperation with the American Library Association.

7-7

for party travel hire a coach

8. Symbolic

Symbolic language is the oldest known form of visual communication. It is also the only language common to the illiterate, the educated, and people of all countries and all races. A symbol of some common experience or emotion provides a universal means of disseminating ideas and exchanging information.

The semi-realistic prehistoric drawings of Egypt and Mesopotamia were the forerunners of the ideographic sign-alphabet, still in use today, though in a much more sophisticated and enlarged version. As a thought-connecting language it is very little affected by distance or time. It spans past and present, present and future. The reason for its linguistic immortality lies in the fact that it is not the language of a single alphabet, but of many alphabets, each designed for a specific purpose: the language of flowers, for instance, for shy or secret lovers to express their feelings when words failed them, or when the exchange of written messages was forbidden; or the handshake which signified the friendship of the stranger who carried no concealed weapon in his hand. Frequently, too, the origin of symbols has become obscured by deliberate manipulation or adaptation to suit a new concept; the swastika and the Christmas tree are both examples of this. Both were part of a pagan ritual, and neither has any connections with its present-day meaning – unless, of course, the 25th century will think that we, too, were as pagan as our distant ancestors seem to us!

Today, when the boundaries of achievement and expanding knowledge have pushed the frontiers of language into the space age, new words and symbols are necessary to describe actual experiences which, hitherto, have only been a figment of the imagination. It is the very nature and immensity of the unlimited power of the imagination that makes a final conclusion either impossible or, at best, a pointless exercise in speculation. And yet there can be little doubt that what exists in the imagination of today is the inevitable of the future. If what once appeared unattainable becomes available, and when the flight of fancy acquires the wings of reality, then surely the language of symbols can translate any idea into a comprehensible form of visual communication, by combining the true with fantasy or facts with the unknown.

One example of the combination of fact and fantasy is the 'Travel is the sign of freedom' poster (8–1; a first prizewinner in the United Kingdom section

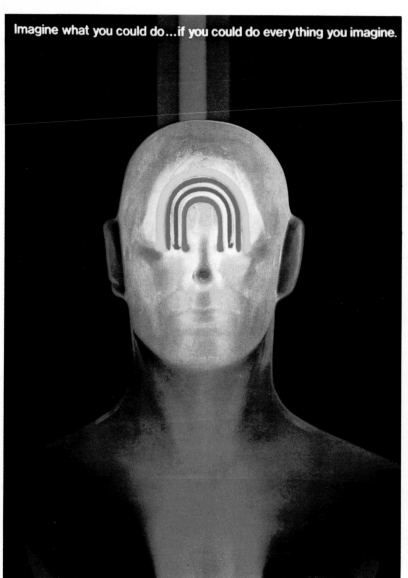

Imagine what you could do...if you could do everything you imagine.

-2

11-5

12-4

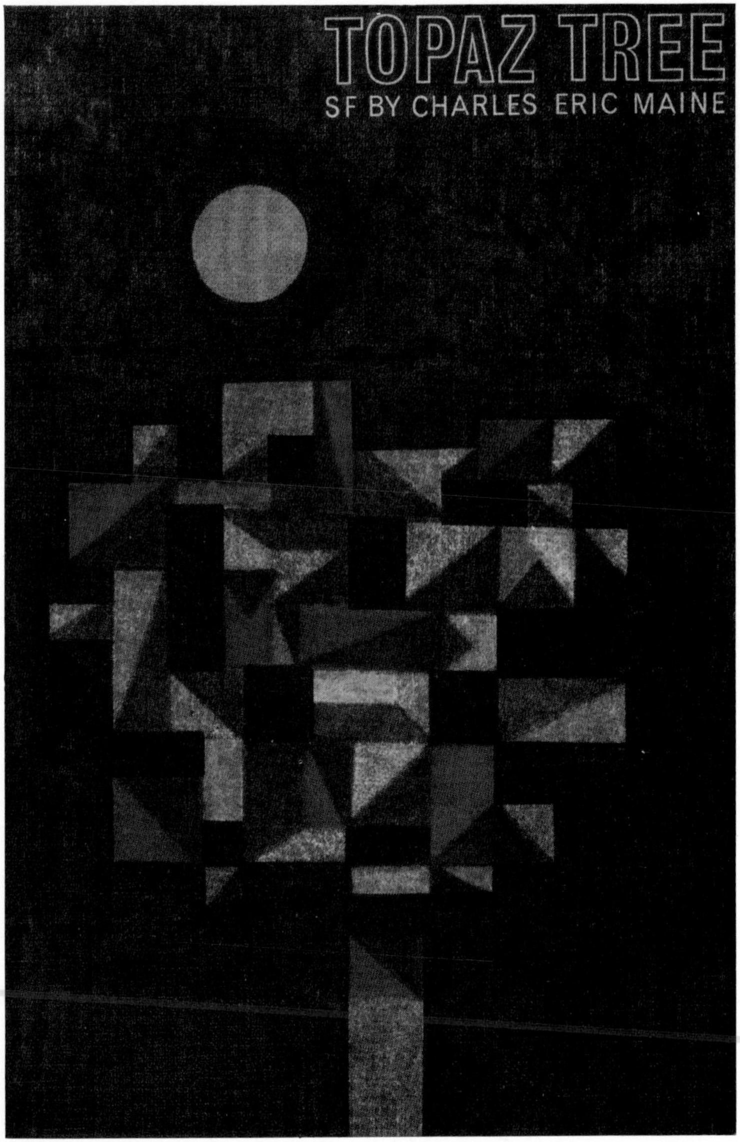

TOPAZ TREE
SF BY CHARLES ERIC MAINE

8-3

PIEKŁO
i NIEBO
czyli komedia z zaświatów
Stanisław Różewicz

8-2

travel is the sign of freedom

8-1

of a competition sponsored by the American magazine *This Week*). The object of this competition was twofold: to encourage travel, free from restrictive and bureaucratic practices, and to promote better understanding between the ordinary citizens of the countries of Western Europe. Obviously 'travel' and 'freedom' were the key words, and the successful solution to this problem revolved round (a) the translation of these words into easily recognizable symbols, and (b) subsequent integration of these symbols into the design. There are, of course, many aspects of travel which lend themselves readily enough to such an aim, but they are all inappropriate in some way. A brief examination produces some interesting results. For a start, suitcases, knapsacks, and travelling bags do not suggest freedom. Instead, they clearly imply some degree of constraint or limitation – the antithesis of freedom. Maps suggest both travel and freedom, but only within a certain confined area. The globe and the Mercator projection of the world were both ruled out because they translate 'travel' into a static negative form; there is a lack of any tangible personal element; and they are rather overworked as symbolic devices. Frontier barriers, raised or broken down, could be interpreted as the aftermath of war, revolution, or invasion. Signposts and arrows are signs of direction. Hitch-hiking could easily be misinterpreted, since it conveys not only the concept of freedom, but also banishment, poverty, lack of suitable transport or roads, a search, a test, an exercise, and military training.

Thus the first key word, which had seemed the most promising, did not produce the expected breakthrough. The second key word – 'freedom' – has no intrinsic connotations with travel, and so was not considered likely to be of any use on its own. Freedom is both relative and ephemeral. It means different things to different people – but to be effective a symbol must have the same meaning for almost everyone. After all, one man's freedom could be another man's prison.

In the end, an inspired solution was arrived at, derived from the old saying 'free as a bird'; and its eminent suitability for the purpose becomes even more obvious with the realization that it has its counterpart in almost any language. Thus the formation of flying wild ducks, symbolizing known fact, and the fantasy of their plumage in the colours of the national flags of the participating countries, encapsulates, simply and effectively, the essence of the message that travel *is* the sign of freedom.

10-1

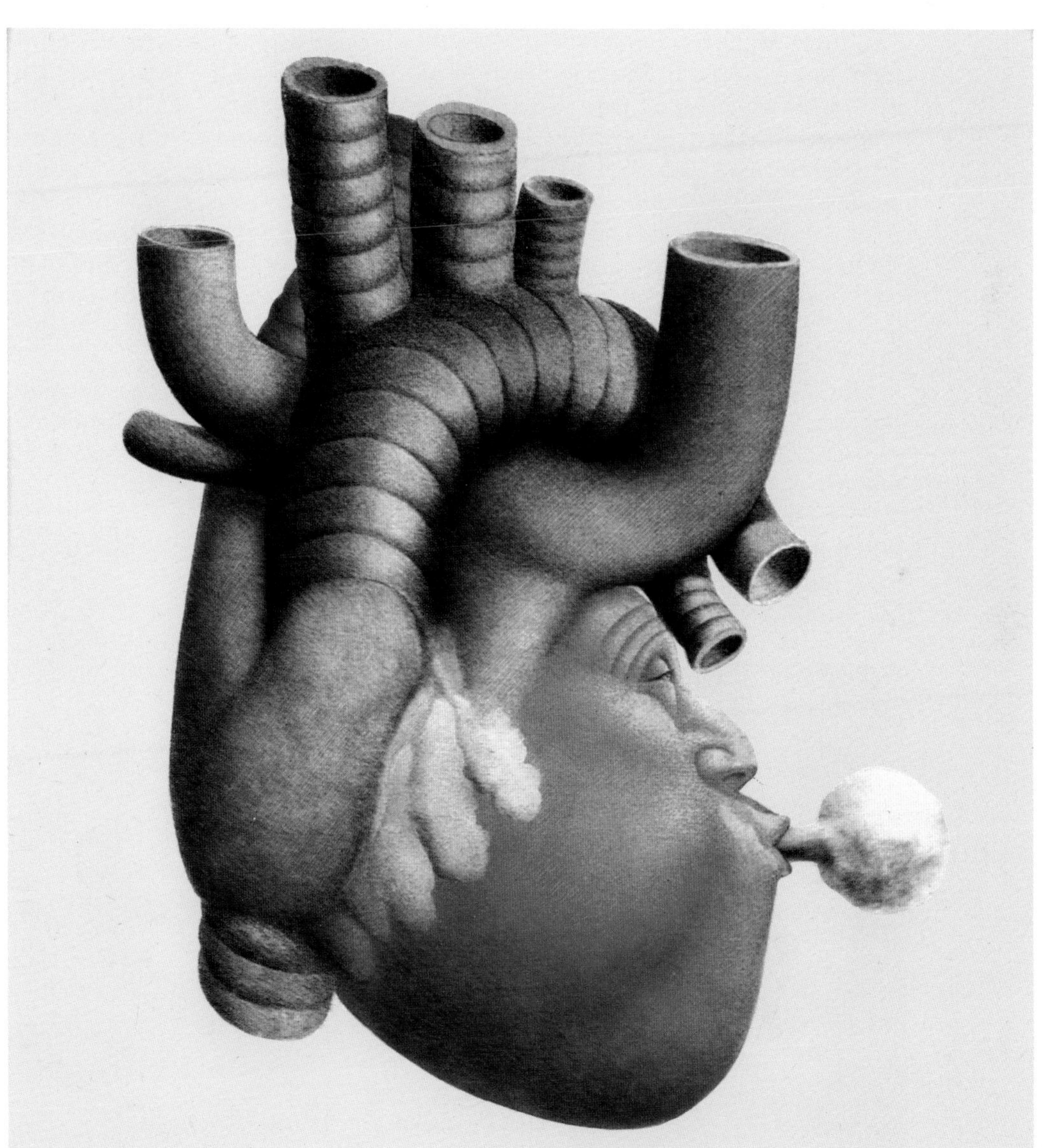

12-2

The cover for a science-fiction novel entitled *Topaz Tree* (8–2) is, on the other hand, an example of the combination of the factual and the unknown. The assumption that such a tree exists somewhere in the galaxy – or, indeed, that it does exist at all – rests exclusively upon the lack of contrary evidence, and is quite irrelevant. The problem of how to symbolize the unknown is reduced to a simple question and decision. If the title of the book is taken as the operative word for the design, should the 'topaz' element be expressed in the shape of the whole tree, or should it be focused on any particular part of it, such as the flowers, fruit, leaves, or trunk? The answer to this question will be largely a matter of personal opinion and subjective preference as to whether the tree or the topaz aspect should be emphasized.

Working on the principle that the more unlikely the unknown, the closer its relation to fact, the foliage of an otherwise conventional tree silhouette is replaced by a cluster of topaz stones. Thus the unknown fact is assimilated into an integrated and convincing symbol.

The remaining examples further underline the variety of characters in the inexhaustible range of the symbolic alphabet, to which more letters are constantly being added.

8-4

8-5

PIRELLI

8-6

karo
express coach services everywhere

8-7

WHIZZ
KIDS
Business Efficiency Exhibition
Olympia. October 2-11

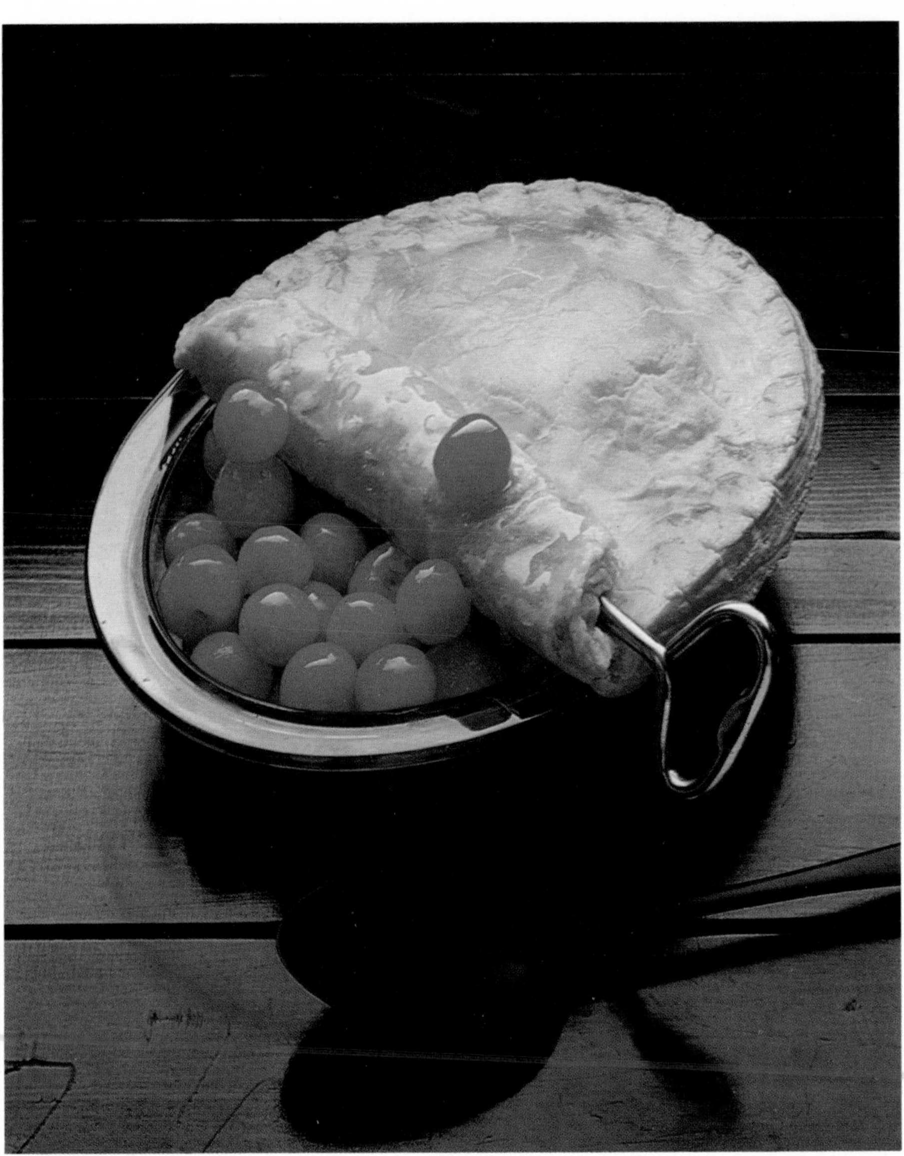

5-1

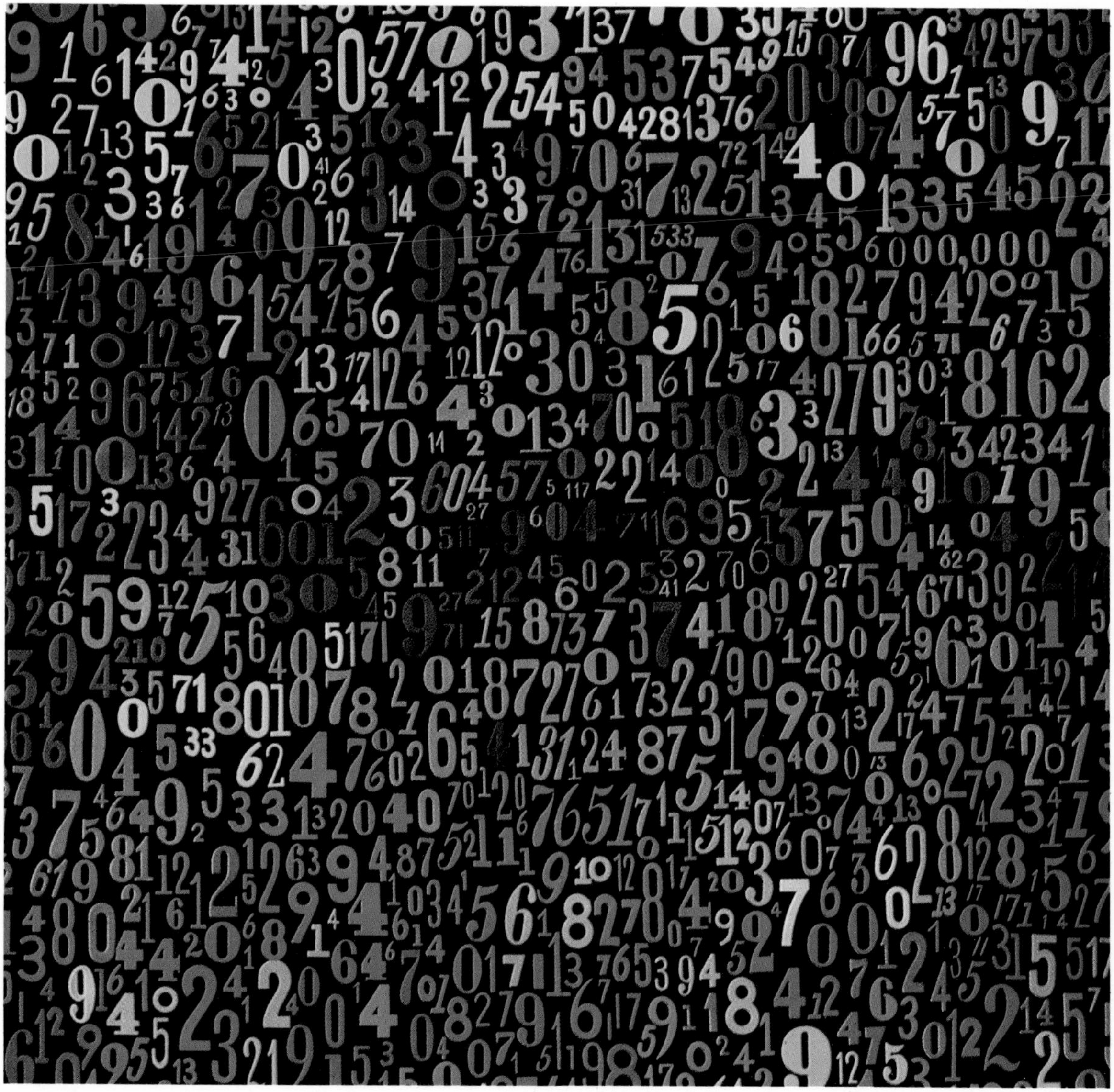

9-3

9. Typographical

Typography, in the opinion of some people, is dry, exact, and creatively unexciting both in itself and as a constituent of graphics. In one sense, such a belief is justified, even if misguided. There are many designs which, although excellent in every other respect, are spoilt because their typography has quite evidently been treated as an afterthought, or as an unavoidable nuisance. On the other hand, the grid system can be used over-zealously, resulting in 'strait-jacketed' visual strangulation.

The fact that typography is the constant thread of all graphic activities is too obvious to need further emphasis. There are currently some six hundred type-faces, for every conceivable occasion and purpose. Each one is a family of twenty-six closely integrated people with a character and individuality of their own. The range of expressions and meanings that can be created or conveyed by sensitive and skilful use of these type-faces is limited only by the creative ability and imagination of the person using them. It should be remembered, too, that typography is not an isolated aspect of graphics, but an integral part of the total design. Each one of those twenty-six characters is a design in itself, capable of adaptation to all forms of imaginative and emotive manipulation. In the words of that advertisement for National Library Week, they can be 'arranged in ways that make you cry, giggle, love, hate, wonder, ponder and understand'. And if that is not enough, they can also be designed to make you act, believe, care, doubt, explore, go, look – and buy. The possibilities are endless: illustrative or informative, implicit or explicit, they are capable of expressing any subject.

However, whatever the style or subject might be, the quintessence of all typography must not be forgotten. To quote Thomas James Cobden-Sanderson: 'The whole duty of typography, as of calligraphy, is to communicate to the imagination, without loss, the thought or image intended to be communicated by the author'. This is not an idea to be aimed at, but a statement of professional responsibility. No thought or idea, however brilliant, can be communicated telepathically to the intended recipient. After all, in the final analysis it is the idea that sells – as, in the words of the 'Tonnage' advertisement (9–1) for Young & Rubicam Advertising: 'Everything depends on the idea. Ideas sell products because – people buy ideas'.

'Next time, read the fine print' is an unequivocally point-blank message. The fine print on the advertisement itself (9–2) reads: 'Next time you see an advertisement that screams about fantastic returns on savings, read the fine print'. The pointed reference to reading the fine print is without a doubt applicable in many other cases – in this case, the opposite message is intended, and it is the *good* news that is contained in the fine print, which, of course, people *will* read.

Your returns on investments might not necessarily be fantastic, but they could easily be rather complex to work out, and you would welcome the opportunity of calculating the net gain quickly and accurately. On the other hand you might be involved with cost accounting, fluctuating cash flow, logarithms, or just plain exponential mathematics – trying to compute the total sum or probability percentages. By stressing the complexity of mathematical calculations, the deliberately exaggerated mass of unrelated numbers on the Olivetti poster for electronic calculators (9–3, page 69) clearly suggests that apparent chaos can be organized, and that an Olivetti calculator is the right machine for the task.

9-1

9-2

2-5

3-7

LONDON

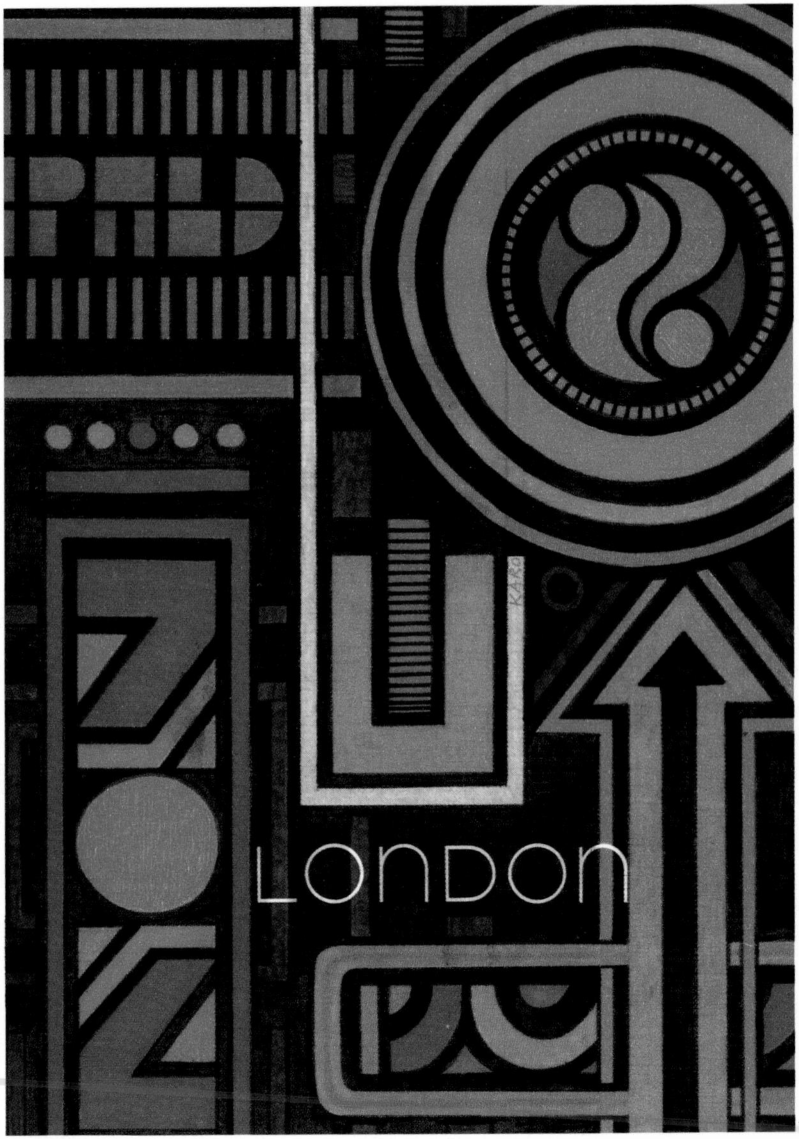

1-

The black and white press advertisement (9–4) 'Questions & Answers by Directomat' presented a different but related problem. Here, the mechanical simplicity and directness succeed in creating a visual definition of an automatic question and answer machine, supplying 120 answers to 120 questions by automation.

The sharp S-bend in the wording 'Pirelli Cintura Safety in Cornering' on a bus poster (9–5) is an excellent example of the use of creative typography as a predominant part of the total design, and as a means of achieving a descriptive solution. The character of the lettering suggests a rigid obstruction or a continuous row of buildings: it emphasizes the dangers inherent in cornering, and simultaneously the dependability of Pirelli tyres.

The Swiss poster 'Salon de l'auto' (9–6) provides another example of imaginative word-manipulation, resulting in successful synthesis of the message via its subject.

The gentle, rolling landscape of the 'Olma' poster for an agricultural fair (9–7) represents yet another application of the typographical method. The undulating fields of letters achieve an almost photographic quality, capturing the essence and the pastoral character of the message.

In conclusion, it should be pointed out that, while the treatment of all these subjects is far from being dry and unexciting, the subjects in themselves are quite prosaic. It is the creative imagination of the designer that has transformed them.

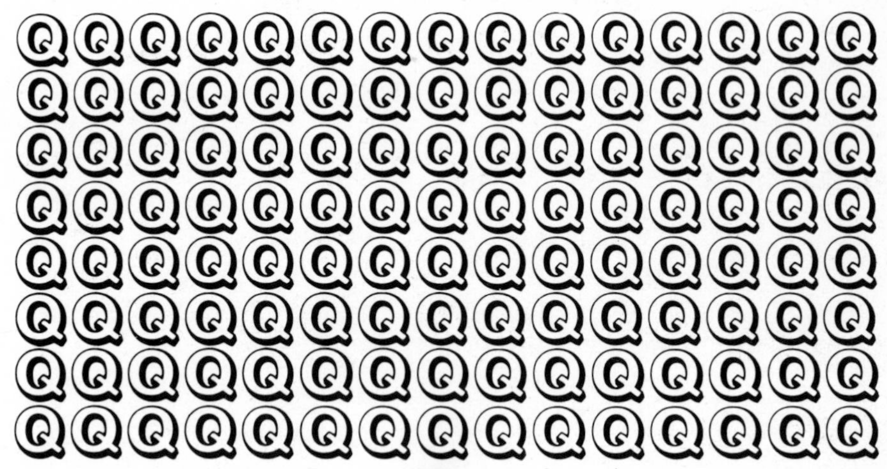

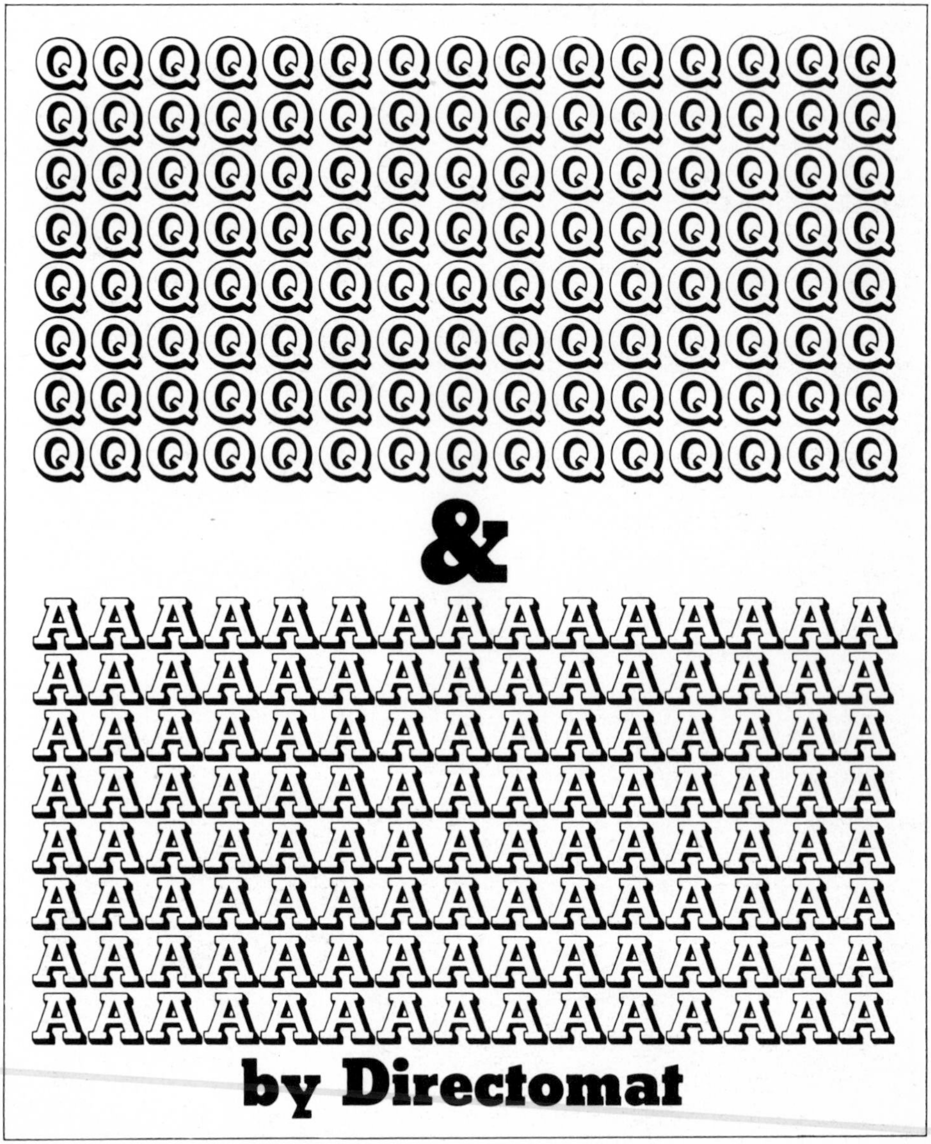

QQQQQQQQQQQQQQQ
QQQQQQQQQQQQQQQ
QQQQQQQQQQQQQQQ
QQQQQQQQQQQQQQQ
QQQQQQQQQQQQQQQ
QQQQQQQQQQQQQQQ
QQQQQQQQQQQQQQQ
QQQQQQQQQQQQQQQ
&
AAAAAAAAAAAAAAA
AAAAAAAAAAAAAAA
AAAAAAAAAAAAAAA
AAAAAAAAAAAAAAA
AAAAAAAAAAAAAAA
AAAAAAAAAAAAAAA
AAAAAAAAAAAAAAA
AAAAAAAAAAAAAAA
by Directomat

9-4

PIRELLI CINTURA
SAFETY IN CORNERING

9-5
9-7

9-6

10. Unusual

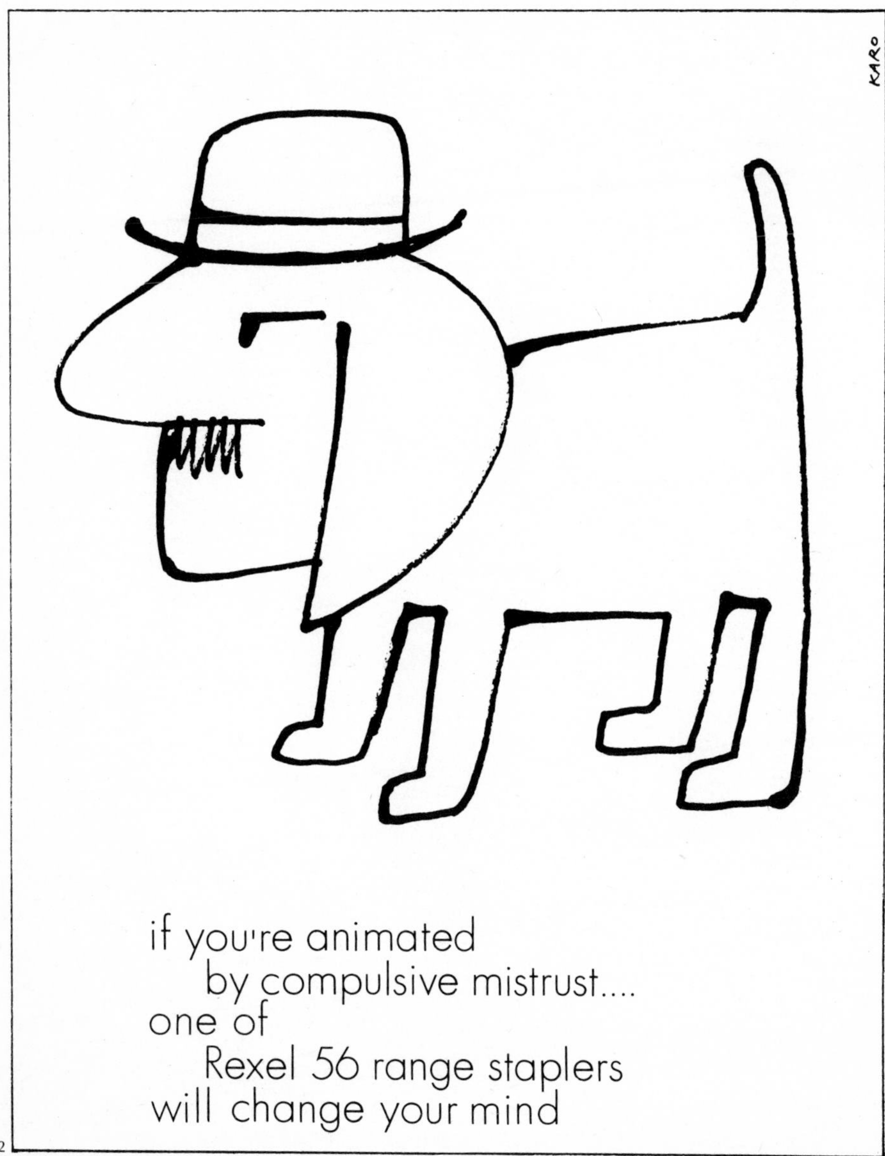
KARO
if you're animated
by compulsive mistrust....
one of
Rexel 56 range staplers
will change your mind

10-2

10-3

Paradoxically, and yet naturally enough, it is often a mundane or orthodox problem which produces an unusual solution. The unusual is not unusual in itself – it is its unexpected, sometimes surrealistic effect in a particular situation that makes it stand out. These examples are typical of their kind, and prove the point that no subject is too dull, or incapable of imaginative solution.

The apparently uninviting problems of how to encourage people to take advertising space in a national daily newspaper, or how to advertise glue, shoes, staplers, and tinned ham, are not ones which readily lend themselves to imaginative rendering. However there are exceptions to the rule, and the circus poster (10–1, page 64) is one of them.

This particular poster was originally designed for a competition, received a second prize, and began to gather the dust peculiar to experiments successful only in the opinion of their creators, Some three years later, during a matinée performance in a continental circus, two tame lions managed a brief escape from their cage – but in those few minutes of freedom they had caused panic amongst the audience, most of whom were young children. No one was hurt, but the ensuing press publicity was more concerned with fiction than facts. The circus's reputation for safety, and the public's confidence in it, had to be restored as quickly and convincingly as possible.

The design is still basically the same as the original, but the second version was deliberately made more light-hearted. It turned out to be a great success: partly because of the juxtaposition of two diametrically opposed but characteristic elements of the circus, but largely because (in the opinion of the designer) it featured a lion – the very animal which had undermined the circus's image, and therefore the only animal that could restore it.

Staplers come in different sizes and shapes. They can be small or large, light or heavy. In the office, in industry, and in the home they are used to staple together two or more pieces of card or paper. What else is there to say about them that is not known, or has not been said before? As a visual problem it was hardly exciting, but when a series of three black and white advertisements aimed at domestic users was requested, it seemed fairly limited too. The client's brief included thorough background information of a general character, and a clear indication that something quite different was wanted.

An examination of the company's wide range of staplers, plus the designer's own experience of rather unorthodox use of four assorted staplers, proved informative enough to suggest a number of clues and possibilities. It also revealed that staplers can be used instead of the more common method of fastening in some fifty different situations: staples can be substituted for pins, safety pins, adhesive tape, paper clips, cotton, string, glue, and nails. Furthermore, using a stapler was frequently less damaging to the article in question, quicker, and more effective – and the staples could be removed if so required.

The conclusion arrived at was a simple, if inevitable one:
(1) The stapler is considerably under-used, because
(2) It is usually bought for only one specific purpose.
(1) and (2) are mutually motivated, but to show any one stapler performing any one of its other known functions would be pointless, because however unusual that function might be, it would only create yet another 'one specific purpose' image. By now the obvious and equally paradoxical solution had emerged (10–2): that the way to show the versatility of a stapler is *not* to show the stapler or what it is capable of.

Summer in the newspaper industry is known as the 'silly season'. That is to say that headlines are made from all kinds of insignificant or trivial stories, which would never appear in print at all, but for the lack of real news items in the slack summer holiday period. The circulation of newspapers drops, and so does the revenue from advertising space. Business doesn't stop because people go on holiday, but it does fluctuate, and most newspapers attempt to overcome this annual problem by offering advertising space at reduced rates. The off-peak discount is advertised by direct mail and, to a lesser extent, in the newspapers themselves.

In either case it must have an attention-getter story or an unusual angle – a typical silly season story of the 'man bites dog' genre, but one that will stand out from the rest. The businessman in the bath tub (10–3) makes that kind of story. No doubt it is as silly to go across the sea in a bath tub as it is to conduct one's business while on holiday – but then it *is* the silly season, after all.

A perfect example of the quintessence of utter simplicity is provided by Savignac's poster for tinned ham (10–4). It is enough to say that it is a brilliant idea, and a superb piece of creative thinking.

If you think that the black cat (10–5) has been persuaded by Savignac's poster that ham is ham, tinned or not, as long as he can get to it – you might be right! At present, however, he is standing on a grand piano which is glued to the ceiling. Whether such an immensely strong glue does in fact exist is, frankly, beside the point. As an advertisement for glue, it is the most imaginative of its kind. Never mind the sceptic who says it cannot be true, or the cynic who asks how many people have a grand piano anyway! The inference is crystal clear.

GRRRRRR! is a tiny female alligator (10–6) disguised as an elegant pair of shoes, and obviously the daughter of very clever parents!

The photographer inside the electric light bulb (10–7) keeps the light burning for many long hours. Being, as he is, one of the top names in advertising photography might explain why he insists on delivering the prints or transparencies personally – normally between 2 and 4 a.m., just before going home.

10-4

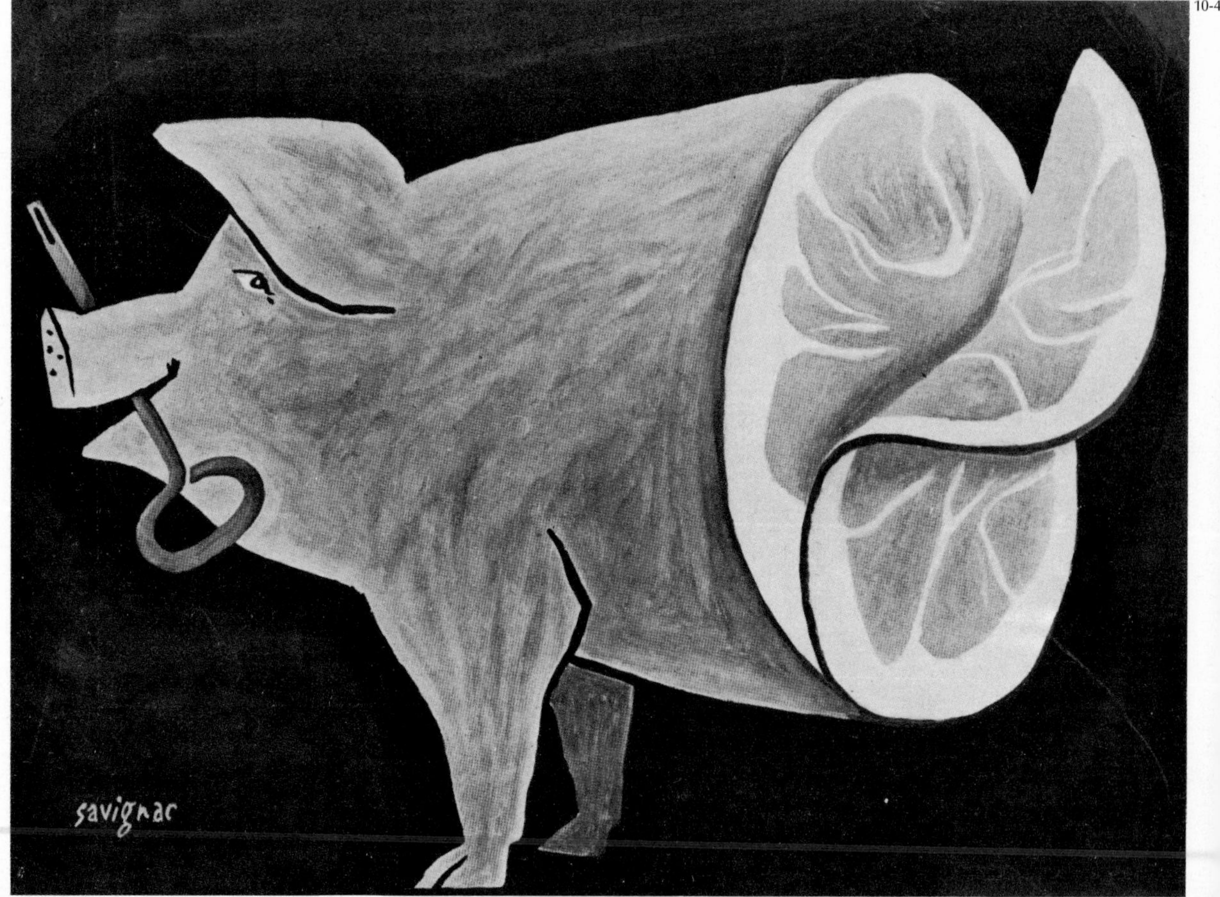

10-5

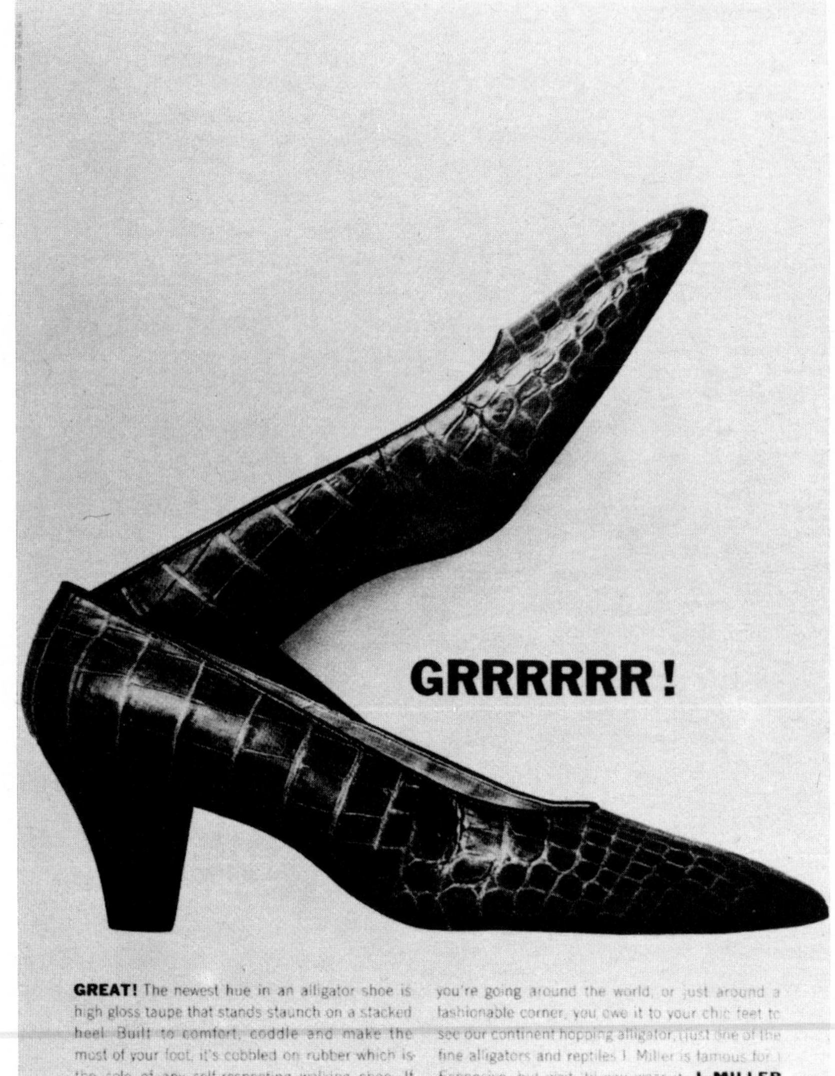
GRRRRRR!
GREAT! The newest hue in an alligator shoe is high gloss taupe that stands staunch on a stacked heel. Built to comfort, coddle and make the most of your foot, it's cobbled on rubber which is the sole of any self-respecting walking shoe. If you're going around the world, or just around a fashionable corner, you owe it to your chic feet to see our continent hopping alligator, (just one of the fine alligators and reptiles I. Miller is famous for.) Expensive, but wait 'til you wear it. I. MILLER

10-6

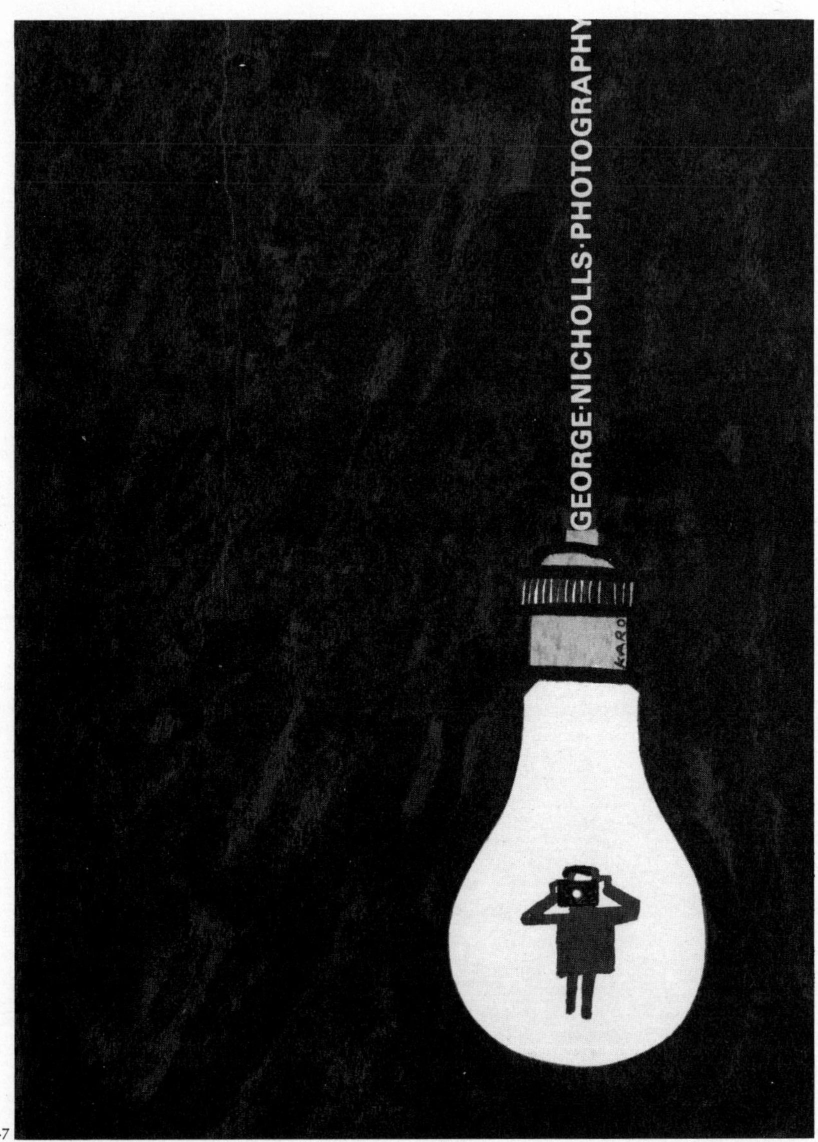

10-7

11. Whimsical

To sell tonic water – which, according to one unreliable source, is said to improve or dilute the gin, depending on how much you have drunk – could be lots of fun. But when you get a client, a writer, and a designer together because all three agree that selling tonic water should be fun, you can be sure it will be. This rare triumvirate lasted long enough to produce several unique and delightful series of advertisements. The client was Schweppes; the designer George Him; and the writer the late Stephen Potter.

Here is an excerpt from the 'University of Schweppshire' series (11–1). 'Report on Drama. The amalgamation of S.H.R.O.U.D.S. and the Foglamps resulted in a successful year, although a modern English play by Schwesker, translated into Rumanian and acted on the circular staircase of the 13th century Tower of All Spirits by 12 bus conductors chosen and rehearsed at random, did not get good notices.'

But time marches on, and a year later Schweppshire became the 'with with-it' series (11–2). Reflecting upon the problems of the day with its usual public-spirited constructiveness, it announced the following: 'To Let. Two-sleeper car in immovable road block continuously held up by permanent repairs to impermanent way. In commanding position on peaceful Schwepton By-Pass By-Pass'. Other attractions included 'special instructional courses provided for those who don't know how to walk. Easy terms . . . L badges provided'. Those were the days!

Today a colour television is nothing like the novelty it used to be. Few, if any, will still remember where the first colour set was installed – or indeed would want to. But credit must be given where it is due. Particularly as it was Schweppshire which transmitted the first colour TV programme (11–3). It went out in 1962, and the colour system, specially designed to be received on four-colour halftone dots, was called Schweppsicolor to perpetuate the name

OBSERVATION PLA RM
JULIUS CÆSAR

of the majority shareholder. Like its numerous followers, it did have some teething troubles: 'T.V. Schweppsicolor encourages music; but everybody agrees that good music is bad camera. Nevertheless it is our aim to make music acceptable to the eye. The question of length is important, and our available periods, of thirteen minutes twelve seconds, make a certain manipulation, i.e. shortening, inevitable. Repeats are out, together with needless echoes of a phrase of the kind which occur somewhat redundantly surely in the first 3 bars of Beethoven's Fifth'. The personnel problem was largely a question of tact: 'choice of soloists with personality is obviously important, but our contralto also has quite a pretty voice . . . . . by special permission of the conductor, the camera occasionally leaves him and pans' – no doubt to admire the string section, since 'to help distinguish them from the second violins, violas have been varnished purple instead of brown'.

These are all excellent examples of prestige advertising: there is no particular message to convey, other than to keep the product in the public eye.

The do-it-yourself fan leaning out of the chest of drawers (11–4) is in fact stuck there – one may well ask what on earth he is doing there in the first place. The attraction of do-it-yourself, as we all know, is very considerable. Leaving aside the saving on labour costs, the opportunity for displaying one's ingenuity and craftsmanship – not to mention the meticulous attention to detail – is practically irresistible. However, many good ideas turn out to be even better when left to the experts. Meanwhile, how does one get out of the drawer, and find out where one went wrong? Sunday is coming, and on Sunday comes the *New York Times*. Section 2 will get the not-so-competent do-it-yourself addict out of his predicament. And maybe when he has read Section 2 he will read the rest of the paper, and become an addict of the *New York Times* too.

Of course, not everybody gets stuck by mistake. Some do it deliberately. A certain Swiss cheese manufacturer produced a Christmas card with a miniscule Santa Claus inside a large sample of his product – to prove that a Christmas card from a Swiss cheese company can be lots of fun (11–5, page 61).

It is hard enough for a manufacturer to make a big name for himself, but it is even more difficult to maintain it. When you *are* known for what you do, people take notice of everything you do. Superior Tube Inc. of the USA is one

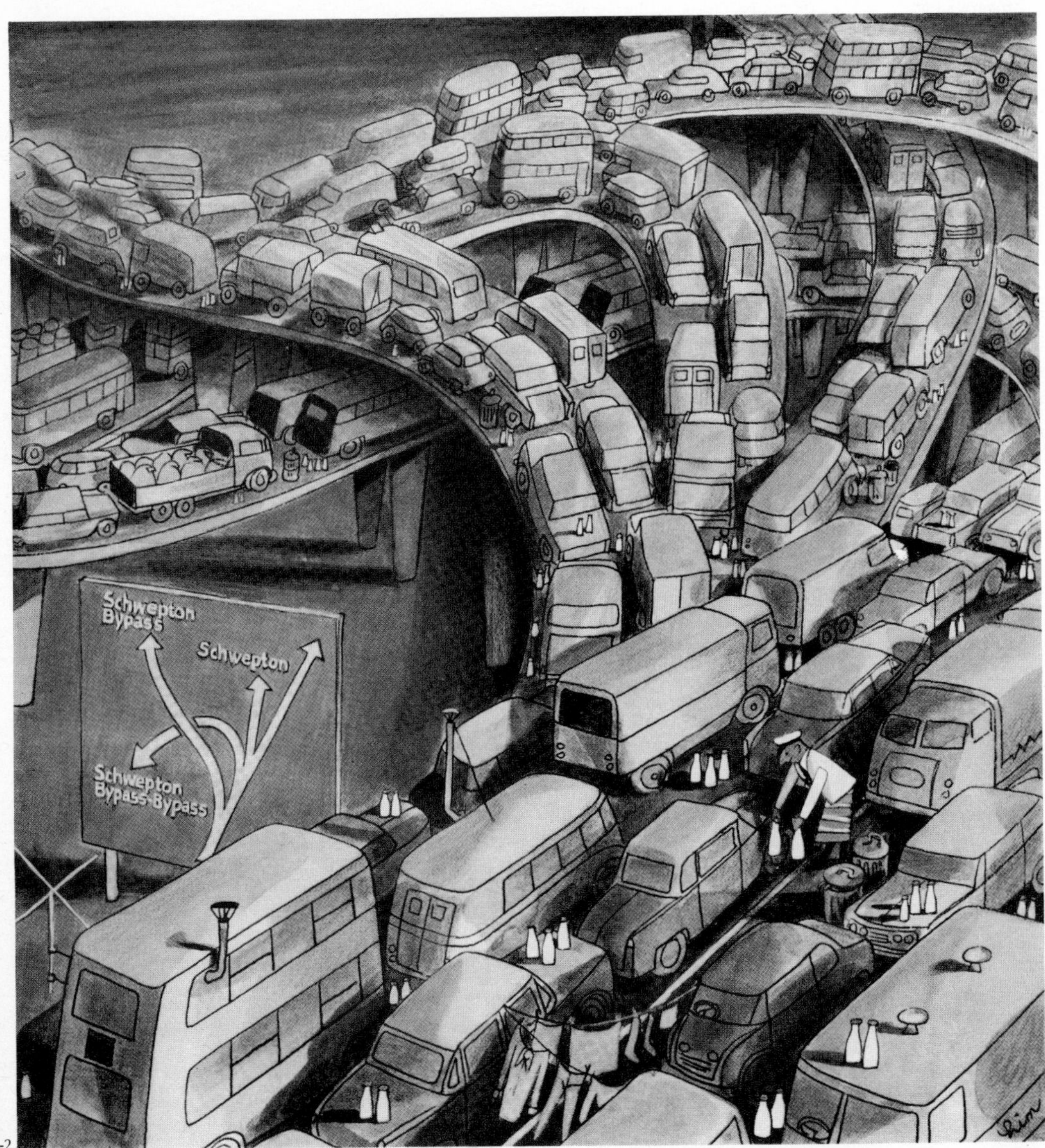

-2

such company, and if, as in this case (11–6), the name happens to stand for quality and precision, every user knows that the product is 'right on specs'. No doubt one of the reasons why the company has a big name in small tubes is because one-sixth of its employees work in quality assurance; not to mention the manner in which the company says it.

For a contrast in subject, but an equal measure of success, take a look at 'CPV are branching out in all directions'. The imaginative brush-tree of André François (11–7) clearly demonstrates that, if the original is born from necessity, then whimsy must be the child of a smile; and that Colman Prentis and Varley have a flair for making creative mountains out of everyday molehills.

11-3

CPV
A.F.
are branching out in all directions
Colman Prentis and Varley Ltd ADVERTISING 34 Grosvenor Street, London. Affiliate offices in Belgium, Canada, Colombia, France, Italy, U.S.A., Venezuela. Associates in 50 other countries.

11-7

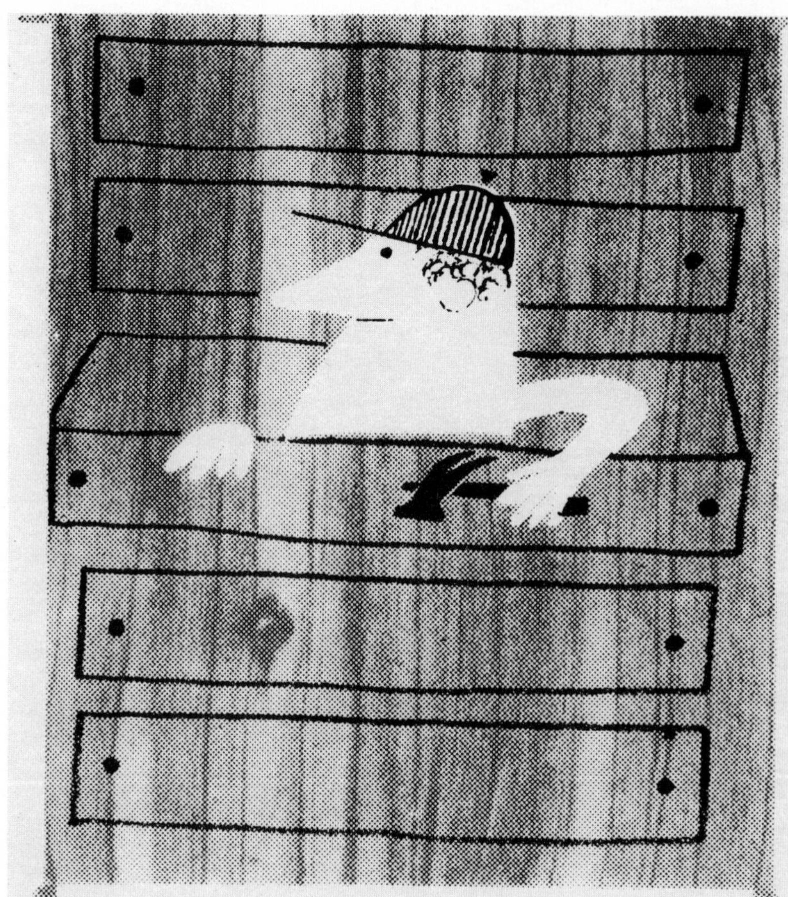
Be sure to read
"DO-IT-YOURSELF"
See Section 2 Sunday

11-4

One sixth of our people work in quality assurance.
When you insist on the big name in small tubing,
you know it will be right on specs. Write for article
reprint on testing procedures.
Superior Tube

11-6

12-1

12. Wordless

12-3

12-5

12-6

12-7

Conclusion

The arguments against advertising in general and the power of advertising in particular continue unabated. The fact that much of advertising is bad and some of it occasionally misleading is obvious enough, as is the aura of misunderstanding which surrounds it. The currently fashionable opinion that advertising is a phenomenon peculiar to the capitalist system defies all the evidence. As someone who has never worked inside an advertising agency, I am sufficiently realistic to point out that selling is, after all, the oldest profession known to mankind, and that advertising is only a relatively new and sophisticated aspect of selling on a very large scale, now made possible by the mass media.

It could be argued, on the basis of much conclusive evidence, that there is no real difference between the effect created by the persuasiveness of an advertisement, and the basic 'unbiased' information. It is the arousal of one's interest in the first place, and the action taken as a result of received information, whatever its form, which alone convert the 'slanted' advertisement or the 'unbiased' facts into something persuasive.

There is in fact very little difference between the 'slanted' advertisement and 'unbiased' information. What difference there is rests upon a very fragile definition of the former as being produced purely in the interest of commerce; and the latter as being produced for the benefit or enlightenment of the public. To sell an idea or a product is, *ipso facto*, a practical application of 'preaching to the converted'. Without a potentially willing buyer there can be no sale.

Leaving aside the question of ethics and definitions, what useful conclusions can be drawn for the graphic designer or student of graphics? At this point it ought perhaps to be mentioned that in terms of complex subjects such as graphics, no final comments are possible. Nevertheless the professional pragmatism so often expounded in this book does not permit any excuses whatsoever, least of all from a confirmed protagonist of creative thought.

My own firm belief that you cannot teach something you could not do yourself might not be particularly appropriate in this context. But it does remind me of the frequently heard and anxiously expressed question: 'How does one become a success?' If there are any golden rules to be followed or tricks to be learnt, then they are outside my knowledge and experience!

Success, when it does arrive, may be the result of ambition and hard work, or a singular opportunity. But in either case the determination to do one's best in any given situation is the decisive factor responsible. According to some, luck must play a very important part because success seems to be synonymous with luck, and vice versa. Jean Cocteau, on his election to the French Academy, was asked by a reporter if he believed in luck. 'Of course I do,' he replied. 'After all, how could you otherwise explain the success of people you don't like?'

Regretfully – or perhaps just as well – I have no morals to pass on, and no lessons to teach. The evidence of what has already been accomplished by others speaks for itself. What those following them will themselves achieve is yet to be seen.

Index of Illustrations

Key
1. Client and Country of Origin
2. Title
3. Designer
4. Artist
5. Art Director
6. Photographer
7. Copywriter
8. Agency

Note. While every effort has been made to trace the names of all those involved in each piece of work illustrated in this book, in some cases this information was not available.

1. Allegorical

1–1 1. Zanders Paper Mill, Germany
2. Ikonolux
3–8. Graphicteam

1–2 1. Siegwerk-Farbenfabrik, Germany
2. Der Regenbogen bringt es
3–8. Not known

1–3 1. British Transport Commission, London
2. Coach tours for everyone
3–4. Jerzy Karo
5. D. Muirhead

1–4 1. National Bus Co., London
2. London
3–4. Jerzy Karo
5. D. Muirhead

1–5 1. Overhead Door Corporation, USA
2. Super Door
3. Ron Sullivan
4. Don Ivan Punchatz
5. Woody Pirtle
6. Glenn Advertising, Dallas, Texas

1–6 1. Allen & Hanburys Ltd., London
2. Dequadin
3–4. Jerzy Karo
5. J. Rimington
8. Haddon's Advertising, London

1–7 1. Geigy, USA
2. Colchicine
4. Paul Davis
5. William Alderisio

2. Direct

2–1 1. Government of Finland
2. Life-meter
3–4. Kyösti Varis

2–2 1. Allen & Hanburys Ltd., London
2. Dequalone
3–4. Jerzy Karo
5. J. Rimington
8. Haddon's Advertising, London

2–3 1. CIBA, USA
2. Triple action
3–4. CIBA Design Unit

2–4 1. Allen & Hanburys Ltd., London
2. For longer lasting breath . . .
3–4. Jerzy Karo
5. J. Rimington
8. Haddon's Advertising, London

2–5 1. British Titan Co., London
2. Colour measurements
3–4. Jerzy Karo
5. L. Miller

2–6 1. Geigy, Switzerland
2. Trix
3–4. Herbert Leupin

2–7 1. Red Cross, Finland
2. Anna apusi auttajille
3–4. Erkki Ruuhinen

3. Dramatic

3–1 1. Central Office of Information, London
2. Your gossip his guide
3–4. Abram Games

3–2 1. National Institute of Mental Health, USA
2. Don't blow it with drugs
3–4. Kurt Haiman

3–3 1. Central Police Directorate, Switzerland
2. Weniger Lärm
3–4. J. Müller-Brockman

3–4 1. *Zoom* magazine, France
2. Contre la pollution de l'oeil
3–6. Roman Cieslewicz

3–5 1. Film Polski, Poland
2. Cena strachu
3–4. Jan Lenica

3–6 1. United Artists, USA
2. Anatomy of a Murder
3–4. Saul Bass
8. National Screen Services

3–7 1. Decca Record Co., London
2. Symphonie fantastique
3–4. Jerzy Karo
5. R. Taylor

4. Emotive

4–1 1. Bell Telephone Co., USA
2. Call your mother. She worries
3–8. Not known

4–2 1. Roche Co., Canada
2. Marital tension
3–4. Stuart Ash
8. Gottschalk and Ash Ltd., Montreal

4–3 1. Center for Studies of Suicide Prevention, USA
2. Suicide
3–4. Theo Welti
8. Donated by Geigy Co.

4–4 1. Government of Israel
2. DP
3–4. Abram Games, London

4–5 1. Campaign against Racial Discrimination, USA
2. Stars and Stripes
3–5. Dick Green
6. Ron Borowski
8. Borowski-Green, Chicago

4–6 1. Industrial Safety Dept., USA
2. Don't take chances
3–4. Abner Graboff

4–7 1. Steiner Salon, London
2. Superiority complex . . .
3. Jerzy Karo
6. Keith Jay
7. Jerzy Karo
8. Haddon's Advertising, London

5. Illustrative

5–1 1. *Supercook* magazine, England
2. Cherry pie
3–6. Don Last

5–2 1. Allen & Hanburys Ltd., London
2. Total relaxation
3–4. Jerzy Karo
8. Haddon's Advertising, London

5–3 1. Hoffmann-la Roche, Switzerland
2. Against vein disease
3–4. Christoph Jenny

5–4 1. Hoffmann-la Roche, Switzerland
2. Flames
3–4. Alberto Solbach
7. P. Forster

5–5 1. Project for a bookshelves manufacturer
2. Pull yourself together
3–4. Tony Mackertich
6–7. Tony Mackertich
8. School of Graphics, Leicester Polytechnic, England

5–6 1. Tool-making Company, Italy
2. New Year News Folder
3. Massimo Robbiano
5. Enzo Careccia
6. Giuseppe Adamo
8. Opit Publicità, Milan

5–7 1. Ice Cream Company, Germany
2. Ice Cream
3–4. Uwe Kracht
7. Axel Forster and P. Moeschlin

6. Impact

6–1 1. Hoffmann-la Roche, Switzerland
2. Romilar
3–8. Not known

6–2 1. Stuttgart Zoo, Germany
2. Zebra
3–4. Hans Lohrer

6–3 1. Allen & Hanburys Ltd., London
2. Whatever the rhinovirus . . .
3–4. Jerzy Karo
8. Haddon's Advertising, London

6–4 1. Aspro-Nicholas Co., France
2. Vite Aspro
3–4. Savignac

6–5 1. Parke-Davis, Germany
2. Molevac
3–8. Not known

6–6 1. Ministry of Transport, USSR
2. 100 . . . 120 . . . 130 . . .
3–4. Saszo Kamenow

6–7 1. Post Office, England
2. Properly packed parcels, please
3–4. Jerzy Karo

7. Implied

7–1 1. King's Men After-shave, USA
2. Why don't you take the 8-45 instead?
3–8. Not known

7–2 1. Western Lithograph Inc., USA
2. Imagine what you could do . . .
3–4. Don Weller

7–3 1. Harvey Probber Inc., USA
2. If your Harvey Probber chair wobbles . . .
3–8. Not known

7–4 1. Ty-phoo Tea Co., England
2. Nobody drinks Ty-phoo tea on the moon . . .
3–4. Jerzy Karo
7. Jerzy Karo

7–5 1. National Library Week, USA
2. abcdef . . .
3–5. Charles Piccirillo
7. Mente Ghertler
8. Doyle, Dane, Bernbach Inc.

7–6 1. Yardley Ltd., London
2. A woman's ammunition . . .
3. Angela Laundels
5. David Cooper
6. John Castle
8. Colman, Prentis & Varley, London

7–7 1. Tilling Group, London
2. Party coach
3–4. Jerzy Karo

8. Symbolic

8–1 1. *This Week* magazine, USA
2. Travel is the sign of freedom
3–4. Jerzy Karo, London

8–2 1. SF Books, England
2. Topaz Tree
3–4. Jerzy Karo

8–3 1. Film company, Poland
2. Pieklo i Niebo
3–4. Jerzy Flisak, Warsaw

8–4 1. *Tribune* newspaper, Switzerland
2. Coffee-pot
3–4. Herbert Leupin

8–5 1. Pirelli, Italy
2. Elephant
3–4. Armando Testa

8–6 1. British Transport Commission, London
2. Express coach
3–4. Jerzy Karo

8–7 1. Project for Business Efficiency Exhibition, England
2. Whizz kids
3–6. John Hine
8. School of Graphics, Leicester Polytechnic, England

9. Typographical

9–1 1. Young & Rubicam, USA
2. Tonnage
3–5. Ottino, Fenga, and Dorelli
8. Young & Rubicam

9–2 1. First Federal Savings and Loan Association, USA
2. Next time, read the fine print
3–5. Dick Henderson
8. Cole, Henderson, Drake Inc., Atlanta, Georgia

9–3 1. Olivetti, Italy
2. Poster for calculating machines
3–4. Giovanni Pintori

9–4 1. Directomat Ltd., London
2. Questions & Answers
3–8. Minale, Tattersfield

9–5 1. Pirelli, England
2. Safety in cornering
3–8. Fletcher, Forbes, Gill, London

9–6 1. Motor Show, Switzerland
2. Salon de l'auto
3–4. Rolf Rappa

9–7 1. Olma, Switzerland
2. Agricultural Fair
3–4. Romano Chichero

10. Unusual

10–1 1. State Circus Co., Germany
2. Lion
3–4. Jerzy Karo

10–2 1. Rexel Co., England
2. If you're animated . . .
3–4. Jerzy Karo
5. Mike Naden
7. Jerzy Karo

10–3 1. *Sunday Times*, London
2. Business in a bath tub
3–5. John Donegan and Mike Norris
7. George Nicholls
8. *Sunday Times*

10–4 1. Ham and Pork Produce, France
2. Tinned ham
3–4. Savignac

10–5 1. Kodak Co., USA
2. Advertisement for glue
3–8. Kodak Studio

10–6 1. I. Miller, USA
2. GRRRRRR!
3–5. Hal Davis
6. Horn/Griner
7. F. Cadwell
8. Jane Trahey Associates

10–7 1. George Nicholls Studio, London
2. Photographer in a light bulb
3–5. Jerzy Karo

11. Whimsical

11–1 } 1. Schweppes, London
11–2 } 2. Schweppshire Series
11–3 } 3–4. George Him
7. Stephen Potter

11–4 1. *The New York Times*, USA
2. Be sure to read . . .
4. Bill Sokol
5. Louis Silverstein and Bill Sokol

11–5 1. Alpine Dairy Co., Switzerland
2. Christmas card
3–5. Mark and Nevosad
8. BKS Werbeagentur

11–6 1. Superior Tube Inc., USA
2. One sixth . . .
4. Saul Mandel
5. Elmer Pizzi
8. Gray & Rogers Inc., Philadelphia

11–7 1. Colman, Prentis & Varley, London
2. CPV are branching out . . .
4. André François
5. Arpad Elfer

12. Wordless

12–1 1. Tinned Sardine Manufacturer France
2. Sardine
3–4. Villemot

12–2 1. Hoechst Co., France
2. Against heart disease
4. Michel Guire-Vaka
5. Agnès Gei
8. Editions Boz, Paris

12–3 1. *Daily News*, USA
2. Daily News
3–8. Not known

12–4 1. Brewers' Association, Switzerland
2. Glass of beer
3–4. Herbert Leupin

12–5 1. Kiefer Shoe Co., Germany
2. Lady's shoe
4–5. H. Michel and Günther Kieser
8. Novum GmbH, Frankfurt am Main

12–6 1. Ministry of Health, Finland
2. Anti-smoking
3–4. Kyösti Varis

12–7 1. Unknown, Finland
2. Peace
3–4. Perti Sainio and Kari Kotka